Devil's Advocates

DEVIL'S ADVOCATES is a series of books devoted to exploring the classics of horror cinema. Contributors to the series come from the fields of teaching, academia, journalism and fiction, but all have one thing in common: a passion for the horror film and a desire to share it with the widest possible audience.

'The admirable Devil's Advocates series is not only essential – and fun – reading for the serious horror fan but should be set texts on any genre course.'
Dr Ian Hunter, Reader in Film Studies, De Montfort University, Leicester

'Auteur Publishing's new Devil's Advocates critiques on individual titles... offer bracingly fresh perspectives from passionate writers. The series will perfectly complement the BFI archive volumes.' **Christopher Fowler,** *Independent on Sunday*

'Devil's Advocates has proven itself more than capable of producing impassioned, intelligent analyses of genre cinema... quickly becoming the go-to guys for intelligent, easily digestible film criticism.' ***Horror Talk.com***

'Auteur Publishing continue the good work of giving serious critical attention to significant horror films.' ***Black Static***

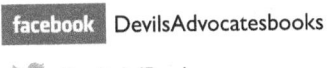

DevilsAdBooks

ALSO AVAILABLE IN THIS SERIES

Antichrist Amy Simmons

Black Sunday Martyn Conterio

The Blair Witch Project Peter Turner

Blood and Black Lace Roberto Curti

Candyman Jon Towlson

Cannibal Holocaust Calum Waddell

Carrie Neil Mitchell

The Company of Wolves James Gracey

Creepshow Simon Brown

The Curse of Frankenstein Marcus K. Harmes

Dead of Night Jez Conolly & David Bates

The Descent James Marriot

The Devils Darren Arnold

Don't Look Now Jessica Gildersleeve

The Fly Emma Westwood

Frenzy Ian Cooper

Halloween Murray Leeder

House of Usher Evert Jan van Leeuwen

In the Mouth of Madness Michael Blyth

It Follows Joshua Grimm

Ju-on The Grudge Marisa Hayes

Let the Right One In Anne Billson

M Samm Deighan

Macbeth Rebekah Owens

The Mummy Doris V. Sutherland

Nosferatu Cristina Massaccesi

Saw Benjamin Poole

Scream Steven West

The Shining Laura Mee

Shivers Luke Aspell

The Silence of the Lambs Barry Forshaw

Suspiria Alexandra Heller-Nicholas

The Texas Chain Saw Massacre James Rose

The Thing Jez Conolly

Twin Peaks: Fire Walk With Me Lindsay Hallam

Witchfinder General Ian Cooper

FORTHCOMING

The Blood on Satan's Claw David Evans-Powell

The Conjuring Kevin Wetmore

Cruising Eugenio Ercolani & Marcus Stiglegger

Peeping Tom Kiri Bloom Walden

[REC] Jim Harper

The Witch Brandon Grafius

Devil's Advocates

Daughters of Darkness

Kat Ellinger

ACKNOWLEDGEMENTS

Special thanks to both Harry Kümel and Danielle Ouimet, without whose generous first-hand insights into the film this book would not have been possible. Additional thanks to Anne Billson, Chris Alexander, Alexander Heller-Nicholas, James Gracey, Heather Drain and Mike White for all your help and support. And, of course, to John Atkinson and Auteur Publishing for making this possible.

DEDICATION

This book is dedicated to the memory of John Karlen (May 28, 1933 – January 22, 2020).

First published in 2020 by
Auteur, an imprint of
Liverpool University Press,
4 Cambridge Street,
Liverpool
L69 7ZU

Series design: Nikki Hamlett at Cassels Design
Set by Cassels Design www.casselsdesign.co.uk

All rights reserved. No part of this publication may be reproduced in any material form (including photocopying or storing in any medium by electronic means and whether or not transiently or incidentally to some other use of this publication) without the permission of the copyright owner.

British Library Cataloguing-in-Publication Data
A catalogue record for this book is available from the British Library

ISBN paperback: 978-1-911325-56-7
ISBN ebook: 978-1-911325-57-4

CONTENTS

Introduction 7

Chapter One: Brides of Dracula 9

Chapter Two: Vampyros Lesbos 31

Chapter Three: Countess Dracula 57

Chapter Four: Twins of Evil 77

Epilogue 93

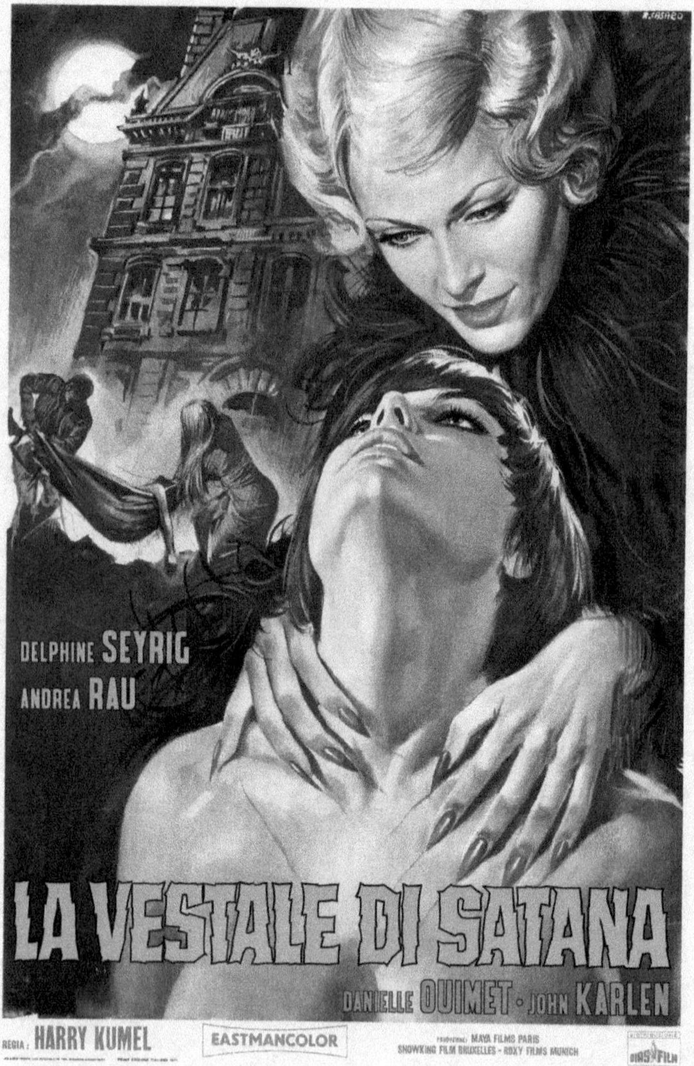

DELPHINE SEYRIG
ANDREA RAU
LA VESTALE DI SATANA
DANIELLE OUIMET · JOHN KARLEN
REGIA: HARRY KUMEL
EASTMANCOLOR
MAYA FILMS PARIS
SNOWKING FILM BRUXELLES - ROXY FILMS MUNICH

INTRODUCTION

Young newly-weds, Valerie (Danielle Ouimet) and Stefan (John Karlen), arrive by train in the middle of the night, at the desolate, windswept coastal town of Ostend, Belgium. The beaches, which are usually teeming with holidaymakers during tourist season, are all but deserted. It is a similar story at the regal-looking hotel the couple pick to spend part of their honeymoon. It's only supposed to be a passing visit though, as Valerie is keen to travel on with her new husband, to England, so she can meet her new mother-in-law, Lady Chiltern. Stefan isn't so enthusiastic and takes steps to delay their plans, insisting they extend their stay at the hotel and rest. He will phone ahead instead, he tells her. His mother needs to get time for the news to sink in. This turns out to be a lie. Stefan is up to no good, and 'mother' is not all that she seems. But then nothing with Stefan is as it seems; he is a man with many dark secrets, some of which Valerie is set to discover within those lonely echoing walls of an off-season hotel, where no one can hear her screams, or the lash of her husband's belt against her tender exposed skin.

On arrival, the couple find they are the only residents of the hotel. But they are soon joined by the enigmatic Countess Elizabeth Bathory (Delphine Seyrig) and her mysterious assistant Ilona (Andrea Rau): a meeting which proves fatal for a couple of members of the party. Bathory is so taken with Valerie that interest soon tumbles into obsession. However, this is no ordinary obsession, and Bathory is no ordinary woman. She is, as the hotel concierge suspects, having recognised her from forty years previously as a visitor to the hotel and seeing she hasn't aged a day, an ancient vampire, who has travelled across Europe for centuries, driven by her thirst for blood and other libertine pursuits.

Harry Kümel's tale of desire, sadism and vampirism is like nothing else from its era. In the years following its release the film has come to be considered a cult classic. Part art film, part Eurocult erotica, *Daughters of Darkness* straddles the divide between high and low. It is a beautiful anomaly, made during a period where lesbian vampire films were in vogue, and in plentiful supply. Yet, it stands out because of its otherness, ironically, in a genre populated with othered outsiders.

Chapter One of this book, 'Brides of Dracula', offers up a comprehensive production history of the film, with exclusive interviews from director Harry Kümel and star Danielle Ouimet, as well as a rundown on all the major cast members, the locations, the music and more. Chapter Two, 'Vampyros Lesbos', turns to compare and contrast, as well as analyse, aspects of the film against its peers and contemporaries within the wider playing field of lesbian vampire cinema in general. Chapter Three probes into the history surrounding the real life serial killer Countess Bathory, as well unveiling several filmic interpretations of her story, with a view to establishing just where *Daughters of Darkness* fits into the overall body of work concerning the infamous Blood Countess. The chapter concludes with an analysis of the sadist and class themes inherent in Kümel's film. Chapter Four contextualises *Daughters of Darkness* within a framework of vampire, Gothic and decadent literature. An epilogue concludes the book by providing further quotes from director Kümel, which illuminate the prospect of a contemporary sequel to his original 1971 film, as well as a brief analysis on the lesbian vampires films that followed much later on, into the 1980s and beyond.

A NOTE ON SOURCES

Unless otherwise indicated, all quotes from Harry Kümel and Danielle Ouimet are from interviews conducted by the author specifically for this book.

Chapter One: Brides of Dracula

Daughters of Darkness started life as a statement to cause a stir. As director Harry Kümel revealed, in an archive interview with Gilbert Verschooten

> It was just a question of getting a young and beautiful couple to fuck as much as possible, with a maximum of blood scenes in between. A real commercial machine! But we thought that wasn't enough, so we also decided to include erotic and chic elements. In that respect we were the precursors of Emmanuelle. (Mathijis 2004: 101)

Elaborating on this, Kümel explains,

> I directed a feature film, which was quite nice, called *Monsieur Hawarden*. It got quite good reviews — not so much in my own country as usual — but in Britain. So, I was very pleased, as you can imagine. And because of this, some young producers here in Belgium, who had worked on some semi-erotic movies and been successful — which was very easy to do at that time — asked me if I could make a film for them, in my style, but with commercial appeal. I said, 'If it's my style it won't be very commercial'. But they gave me the go ahead anyway. I didn't have any idea what the film was going to be about but knew it should have blood, violence, and be erotic, because these were the ingredients for a commercial film at the time.

The director's previous feature film *Monsieur Hawarden* (1968) is something of a spiritual cousin to *Daughters of Darkness* in many respects. The Belgian-Dutch co-production was shot on a very modest budget of 600,000 Netherlands Antillean Guilder (around £24,000). Despite the financial constraints, Kümel's ability to capture mood and atmosphere, even from a limited cast and locations, shines through. The story focuses on the mysterious Monsieur Hawarden, who travels with his companion and maid, Victorine, to a remote country house for solitude. The servants of the house speculate over why the man never comes out of his room. They initially wonder if he could be sick, and puzzle over the instructions they have been given to leave him in peace. As the plot develops it becomes apparent the new arrivals are concealing something. Monsieur Hawarden is actually a woman in disguise, hiding from a terrible secret from her past. Kümel makes great use of the rural locations, lengthy dialogue scenes and black-and-white photography and as a result crafts a cultured, brooding piece of Gothic drama, which defies its low-budget origins.

Where *Monsieur Hawarden* synchronises with *Daughters of Darkness* is in its focus on female companionship and dark secrets. Both films depict a pair of women forced to live a nomadic lifestyle, running from something they don't want anyone else to find out about. Because of this unspeakable thing, a relationship develops between the women, which breaks the boundaries of conventional friendship. The alliance between Hawarden and her maid is founded on more than just the bond between master and servant, as is the companionship between Bathory and Ilona in *Daughters of Darkness*. There are many scenes where Hawarden is shown watching Victorine through her window where it is insinuated within the context of things left unspoken that the older woman has a romantic yearning for her maid. This said, it is made clear in the narrative the women do not share a bed. During other moments, the true nature of their obvious deep connection remains ambiguous; for example the women are seen embracing from time to time and the manner in which they hold each other displays sensuality and tenderness usually reserved for lovers. When Victorine finds a male lover, and ultimately attempts to leave her master, things turn sour with jealousy.

The film is a rare early example of the director's work. Very little is known about his other films by those outside of his native Belgium. Ernest Mathijs gives some vital context with which to frame the director's seminal years in *The Cinema of the Low Countries*. The author states,

> ...when he was still a teenager Kümel (born in Antwerp in 1940), joined SCM, the small film group in Mortsel. He started making short films in 1953 and by the end of the 1950s had directed a series of seven shorts. In 1958 he co-founded with Rick Kuypers, 'Film 58', a collective that set out to renew Belgian cinema. Kümel never attended film school but from 1959 on he began to write scripts for other directors... and directed more professional shorts. Of these *Anna la Bonne* (1959) based on a poem by Jean Cocteau, and *Pandora* (1960)... are still regarded as some of the most mature and promising shorts in Belgian cinema history. Between 1961 and 1965 Kümel mainly worked for the public broadcast BRT, directing for the film review show *Premiere*. Among the reports he directed were portraits of John Huston, Roman Polanski and Vincente Minnelli... He also wrote for magazines, *Films & Televisie* and *Skoop*. (Mathijis 2004: 99)

With many of these early shorts impossible to view outside of Belgium it is difficult to gauge their quality or content. From the information provided by Mathijs the one thing that does become obvious immediately is that Kümel was serious about his craft, even as a teenager. He was also working in a cultural climate which would help foster creativity and innovation in his own cinema. One of the few easily available shorts from this period, his 1965 film *De grafbewaker* (*The Warden of the Tomb*, which is an adaptation of Franz Kafka's play) is an extremely interesting example of his imaginative take on Gothic cinema, not least for the way in which it demonstrates the director's obvious proclivity for dealing with dark or morbid themes, but also because it showcases his ability to think outside of the box when it comes to creating something quite magical out of relatively little resources. The story, as with the original play, concerns a tomb warden outlining the last thirty years of his life to one of his superiors, as he describes how he has spent every night for the past three decades fighting with ghosts, to prevent them from leaving their final resting place. The film, also shot in black-and-white like *Monsieur Hawarden*, with an extremely limited cast — most of the 'action' takes place around just two characters talking — relies completely on dialogue to paint its grim picture, which was an art Kümel had perfected by the time it came to make *Daughters of Darkness*.

By the 1970s Kümel had fully developed his craft. The director had become disenfranchised with his native film industry, which he felt was rife with snobbery, fuelled by a widespread obsession with the auteur school of filmmaking. He wanted to kick back at the system he believed had been unfair to his earlier projects. So, while *Monsieur Hawarden* and *De grafbewaker* embraced dark elements, the director decided his next picture was going to go all out to inflict disgust and terror. He wanted to do something 'nasty'.

The inspiration for one of the most incredible vampire films ever made came completely by chance, as Kümel explains:

> I went ahead, and went for a walk in Brussels and hit upon a newspaper seller. There was a magazine called Historia, and on the cover was a report of a renaissance lady subtitled The Bloody Countess, which turned out to be about Countess Elizabeth Bathory. It took my fancy, so I bought it and read the article, which was quite long. Afterwards I went back to the producers and said, 'well my subject... it has blood... it

has eroticism... it has violence… it has 800 virgins, murdered'. They were surprised, as you can imagine, and said, 'oh no we can't do that, we have no budget for a costume movie!'. When you talk to producers about a period movie they always say 'oh, it's too expensive!'. It's as if we don't have to put people from our time in a costume. It's very silly. You rent. In Britain, for example, you can rent any costume you want, far cheaper than buying modern suits or dresses. If you want to dress people well, it costs a lot. However, the 800 virgins, that was a lot. It was before digital. So I said, 'Well what about if all that blood she drank, to remain young, had made her into a vampire? Hundreds of years later she would still be living. Then the film could take place now, as she would be roaming the earth, looking for virgins; finding them would have become more and more difficult in our time'. They said, 'oh that's a very good idea. Let's develop it.' So, I went with one of the producers and sat down at the table. During three days and three nights we developed a story, which was a rough draft, more or less, of what *Daughters of Darkness* became.

Daughters of Darkness encompasses many aspects of classic literature and culture. It is because of this the film has continued to prove so alluring to cinephiles. However, Kümel is coy about his references; when asked how he developed the story, he explains:

> I read books, like *Valentine Penrose*, before we sat down to write the script of course. It was difficult to have references at that time because it involved going to a public library, not like now when you open Google and you can find all the information you would ever want. I had read Sheridan Le Fanu's *Carmilla* long before. But I wasn't aware of Le Fanu, consciously, when we were writing. Of course, because of the slightly lesbian aspect of the story it does get connected, but that was not something that was in the back of our minds. All we had in our heads was creating as many erotic scenes as possible.

With a script in place the production was approved, and funding was arranged from a number of international territories making it a Belgian/French/Italian/German co-production. The overall budget was set at $750,000 — which included a $45.000 investment from America — and the rest of the budget was split between Belgium (40%), France, Italy and Germany (20% each). The Italian investors would pull out before the film was completed, with Belgium, France and Germany picking up the shortfall.

CASTING

DELPHINE SEYRIG

It almost goes without saying that a huge part of the magic and appeal of *Daughters of Darkness* is down to leading star Delphine Seyrig and her sublime performance as Countess Elizabeth Bathory. If there is one thing Kümel is quite clear on it is that he wanted her from the start and would not have accepted any other star:

> I would've only made the film with Delphine Seyrig in the main part. That was my condition for making the movie. If she wasn't in it, I wouldn't have made the film. I felt the combination of the type of story and using a special star, or let's say a novelty star, would prove explosive. I think that has proven to be true over the years. Everybody sees that. Delphine said to me once, 'If I am remembered in cinema, it's because of your film'. She was amazing, a great actress. And great actresses enjoy challenges. It's different now. Now, what they find challenging is to pee on their protagonists. But that's not daring, of course. It's just silly... I knew her of course, she was a memorable protagonist of a great director, also a friend of mine, Alain Resnais. He pushed her to

do the role. She always said if it wasn't for Alain, she would have hesitated. He was instrumental in having her doing the part. The first time I met Delphine was at the theatre, in France where she was playing in Paris, extremely avant garde theatre. It was there that I saw that the French had no admiration for their actors, because her dressing room was dismal and she was the star of the show. I couldn't understand why the French do not admire theatre, not in that sense. They are not like the British, certainly.

It was Seyrig's background in theatre, especially her performances in the plays of Harold Pinter, which impressed the director the most.[1] Kümel is on record comparing the star to Dame Maggie Smith, as well as other leading ladies of her time and place, such as Simone Signoret, ultimately hailing, quite rightfully, Seyrig as one of the greats of French theatre and cinema.

When asked about working with the star, Kümel replies,

> Oh I loved, loved, loved her, of course! A good actor, like Delphine, comes prepared on the set. You don't have to do a lot. You just have to indicate how they must move, their place in the scene, their place in the story, and remind them how to connect with what they are doing. And then they act. Good actors are not 'motivated' [Kümel's reference here relates to method acting]. It reminds me of the famous story, of Ingrid Bergman and Alfred Hitchcock. When she came to Hitchcock asking, 'What is my motivation?' Hitchcock answered truthfully 'Ingrid you are not paid to be motivated, you are paid to act... so act!' Bergman replied, 'but I don't feel it, I must feel it'. And he said, 'Ingrid, fake it'. Faking it is an actor's job, and Delphine knew this very well.

It hardly comes as any surprise that Delphine Seyrig was so professional when you consider her pedigree prior to working on *Daughters of Darkness*. The French actress was born in Lebanon in 1932 (making her 39 years old when she came to work for Kümel). After initially studying acting in France at Comédie de Saint-Étienne as a young woman, she moved to New York and spent time at the prestigious Actors Studio. While in New York she met French director Alain Resnais, who cast her in *Last Year at Marienbad* (*L'Année dernière à Marienbad*, 1961), the film which launched Seyrig's career in cinema as an important name on the French arthouse circuit. Prior to this she had featured in an American short, Beat Generation film *Pull My Daisy* (1959), which was written and directed Jack Kerouac. Following the success of *Last Year at Marienbad*, the actress returned to work with Renais for *Muriel, or the Time of a Return* (*Muriel ou le Temps d'un retour*, 1963), before going on to play major and minor (yet always fascinating and memorable) roles for directors including François Truffaut, William Klein, Luis Buñuel, Joseph Losey, and, during the latter end of her career, feminist filmmakers Chantal Akerman and Marguerite Duras. Eventually she turned her own hand to directing, making a feature-length documentary on the objectification of actresses in the film industry, *Be Pretty and Shut Up* (*Sois belle et tais-toi*, 1981). The actress also directed two short films *Maso et Miso vont en bateau* (1975) and *Scum Manifesto* (1976).

As anyone who has witnessed Seyrig's performance in Chantal Akerman's *Jeanne Dielman, 23 quai du Commerce, 1080 Bruxelles* (1975) can testify, there was no-one quite like her, and nor is it likely there ever will be. Akerman's film, which runs well in excess of three hours, focuses on the daily chores of a housewife, who turns tricks as a prostitute to make ends meet. The film is completely devoid of the usual erotic connotations involved in this kind of narrative. Instead, Akerman presents the titular Dielman involved mainly in mundane domestic chores; peeling potatoes, preparing meat, scrubbing her bathtub with Ajax, pottering around her pristine compact apartment. Literally nothing of major note happens, until the very end. This is testament to the actress's immense talent. The exercise becomes utterly absorbing through her performance. In everything she turned her hand to, whether it was the dowdy middle-aged stepmother in *Muriel, or the Time of a Return*, glamour wife turned seductress of younger men in *Stolen Kisses* (1968), the mysterious women of *Last Year at Marienbad* and *Baxter, Vera Baxter* (1977), or even dressed as a superhero in a shiny leotard for William Klein's *Mr Freedom* (1969), no matter what she did, she was always no less than brilliant. Kümel elaborates:

> With Delphine, you could just say to her, 'be this, or be that', and, as a very intelligent actor, she would do it. She loved me to position her. She also knew how to make her performance aesthetically interesting. That's why she was interesting. Of course, she always consulted with me on where she would put her pauses. She had a very interesting way of placing extremely conscious pauses and intonations into her speech. 'Where shall I put the intonation on this word, or this word, and what do you think if I put a pause on that word?' And that kind of normal thing that good actors know. That is, just to talk. How to do it technically. It's all technique, nothing

more. The same way you put someone on the right, or on the left in the screen, to indicate whether they are in a dominant or submissive situation. It is nothing magic, it is nothing special. It's something, which, if you are a professional you know *how* to do in cinema. I mean, it's just a job. Delphine was a professional.

Fellow *Daughters of Darkness* co-star Danielle Ouimet had a similarly positive experience and saw working with the French star as one of the highlights on an otherwise gruelling shoot. Ouimet recounts her fond memories of Seyrig:

> Delphine Seyrig was really someone incredible. She was a darling. Like a mother to me. Because she realised that I had no experience. In my previous film in Canada, *Valerie*, I was taking the metro and wearing my own clothes to do the film. Suddenly here I am in a production where they take me with a chauffeur in the morning. It was really something quite different. I laugh about it today but at the time I felt very bad about that. Delphine, she realised that I needed to have someone to support me. I could do it, if I was helped or supported by someone with experience like she had. So what she did was so cute, so marvellous. She would say to me, 'Oh, Danielle do you have time to practise a bit? I don't feel comfortable in this scene, can you help me?' And so we would rehearse [laughs]. I know perfectly well it was for me.

DANIELLE OUIMET

French-Canadian actress Danielle Ouimet, who plays the film's ingénue Valerie, as previously stated, came to *Daughters of Darkness* with very little experience acting in feature films, having made just two films previously, both directed by Denis Héroux and released in Ouimet's home country, where they were commercially successful. The films in question, *Valerie* (1969) and *Initiation* (1970), were sex-heavy and involved plenty of nudity. Therefore, the actress was not daunted by the potential of appearing naked for Kümel for his vampire film. For Ouimet, the opportunity to take part in an international project represented an adventure. She remembers the experience vividly and also recounts her experience of stripping down for her part:

> When I did my first two films I went to the film festival in Cannes. I was asked to go because the producers at Cinepix wanted me to be a success. They wanted me to

work in different things. So they presented me to a French producer who hired me for *Daughters of Darkness*. I realised later on, the director Harry Kümel didn't exactly want to have me. But money talks. Since Canada was ready to give a lot of money, to get the distribution of the film, they were also paying my fees, they took me. So, here I am going to France for my third film and I was very happy to do so. It wasn't the first time I had been to Europe. Actually I love to travel and I was there a few times there before. But it was the first time I was working with people outside of Quebec. But the travel, as a Gemini, it was a plus! It's the most wonderful thing that you can find. I still do, once in awhile. I travel for work, not in the film industry anymore, but other fields. And I love every second. I love to explore. I love everything about being around the world.

Before, when I did *Valerie* and *Initiation* there was a lot of nudity. Everyone says 'Oh my god, how did you feel?' Well, it was crazy fun! You know, for two minutes you don't like having everyone's eyes on you. The set is also closed to two or three people. But still it's fun, like I said. In *Valerie* I had a scene where I'm supposed to be happy. I am bathing in a lake where I was freezing! They had to break the ice before putting me in the water. And they asked me not breathe, because of the condensation. But, the result is that you see a girl who is so happy to be in the water, but it's not true! That's the fun part, when you see how it's made. That's how I remember the scene from *Daughters of Darkness*, where Stefan has his wrist slashed. I remember the glass top, which was in two parts, there was a pump that was supposed to throw some blood around. But we could never stop the pump and it was really, really flying everywhere! We had to change clothes, because it was splashing everywhere. When you see that, it's fun. You don't stop to think about the fact that on the screen it's going to be terrible.

Ouimet's lack of experience did cause friction between her and Kümel, and the production was plagued with arguments, which finally exploded with a violent outburst on the part of the director. Being shut away in a dark hotel for weeks on end, with very little contact with outsiders, took its toll on the performers. The inexperienced actress found this part of the production difficult, as we will see in her later stories surrounding the film.

DEVIL'S ADVOCATES

JOHN KARLEN

Although actress Ouimet felt out of her depth during certain moments of the production, she did find allies with her co-stars, Delphine Seyrig and John Karlen, who played her on-screen husband Stefan. Karlen was brought to the film through the American funding (Gemini Pictures International), off the back of his success in Dan Curtis' supernatural 'soap opera' *Dark Shadows*, which ran from 1966-1971. The series amassed a respectable 1,248 episodes in its life span, and finished up the year Karlen starred in *Daughters of Darkness*. Over the course of the series the actor played several characters, including, most notably, thief turned slave to a vampire master Barnabas Collins, named Willie Loomis, which was a role he would resurrect for the first of two film adaptations: *House of Dark Shadows* (1970). Karlen then starred as a completely different character, Alex Jenkins, for the filmic sequel, *Night of Dark Shadows*, released the same year as *Daughters of Darkness*. In its time the *Dark Shadows* franchise was incredibly popular. The show embraced — much like its modern-day successor of sorts, *True Blood* — various aspects of Gothic literature, and created a world of witches, ghosts, vampires and other supernatural creatures, in a universe packed with magical realism. Karlen's appearance in *Daughters of Darkness* made the film more appealing to international investors. The star was already 38 years old when he came to the production, but starring as newlywed Stefan, a character supposedly much younger than this. The actor's age didn't particularly impress director Kümel:

> We had American financiers and they sent us John Karlen. In fact, I wanted Malcolm McDowell for the part, but he refused. So they sent us John Karlen because he had played in the television series *Dark Shadows*... Before they sent him, they sent promotional photos of him, where he was probably 20 years old. He was long, long, long past 20. When I saw him for the first time I had the shock of my life because he was not this fresh young man that I expected!

Shocks aside, Karlen brings a maturity to his role which suits the character. The actor altered his native Brooklyn accent — heard most prominently in his later major role as husband Harvey in hit television show *Cagney and Lacey* — to sound more European. The effect works. In an audio commentary for a previous Blu-ray release he has acknowledged that people assumed he was dubbed for his part, which wasn't the case.

Like his co-star Seyrig, Karlen also came to his role with a wealth of experience on the stage. Stefan is an incredibly tense, dark and complicated character, which called for a demanding performance.

Co-star Ouimet thought very highly of Karlen. Commenting on the scene in which Stefan beats Valerie, she recalls her time working with the actor:

> I remember the scene where he hits me. He suddenly just realised he was an actor and he decided to do it for real. My god! And he said to me, 'No I won't do it for real. I will smash on the bed. You won't see it'. But he got so carried away I received two or three slaps! Oh my god! We didn't want to stop because, well, we wanted it to be finished and we weren't going to do it again. I remember he wanted to be very hard looking. So, he was smashing on the bed, and looking angry. But there were a few blows went directly on my ass because he was carried away!

When asked about the actor's intensity and her experience working with him, Ouimet continues,

> He's always intense. He's intense in real life. He was very protective of me also. Like both of them. Delphine, and him, they were surrounding me and protecting me. It's unbelievable. I guess that most of the film works because of the fact that we were close that way. When you lack experience, like I did, the only way of doing it is to be completely at the mercy of those who are surrounding you, and helping you. I am a good listener. When I know my line, I just look at the person and answer. But instead of trying to play it, I do it. I live it. It's because it's the only way to do it, otherwise, it might go wrong. It might sound weird. And when some of my lines were sounding weird, it was because I was inexperienced. I had someone like Delphine, to tell me 'Hey, let's practice a bit'. And by doing so, it was falling into place. They [Karlen and Seyrig] were very pleasant. It is one of the best films, family-wise, that I have worked on and I did seventeen films.

> When you are in a film you have to be close. People ask, 'Do you fall in love with those who are around you?' Is it easy to fall in love. I do think it is very possible. Because you eat together; you go to bed at the same time; you get up at the same time; you get your make-up at the same time; you talk about your family. When you

are waiting on the set you are laughing together, because you have to laugh, otherwise it's too heavy if not. You're so much into one another. Closer than that. And it has to show in the production. Mind you, there were twenty people around. But the four of us [Seyrig, Karlen and Andrea Rau, who plays Ilona], we were together all the time. Except for Andrea, the German, who was there not that often. We were always together. It puts you in the position where you can only be friendly. When I talked to John Karlen, and we are still friends even now, about five years ago, he was so kind to me. It very important to be a family when you do a film. You know you are going to have nudity. And nudity for the first five minutes is very uncomfortable, but after that it's technical.

ANDREA RAU

German actress Andrea Rau came to *Daughters of Darkness* via Roxy Films, a German company founded in the 1950s on the back of producing a number of melodramas but which had moved into sex comedies by the 1970s. The company also co-produced notable works such as Jess Franco's *Venus in Furs* (1969) and Rainer Werner Fassbinder's *Lili Marleen* (1981) in amongst their diverse catalogue of films. As Kümel explains,

> We had a German, Andrea Rau. The German producer said 'We need to have a look at this girl'. She was playing at the time in erotic movies, semi-pornographic movies. I went to see her in one of her films, which was showing in that kind of cinema, the kind which showed X-rated movies, and that was the first time I saw her. The funny part, the first image I got of her was she came out of the water. At that time you were not allowed to show frontal nudity in Belgium. So, the distributors used felt pen, and they blotted out every image where you had frontal nudity. So, when she came out, it looked like a swarm of bees in front her. That was very funny. And that was the first image I ever had of her. But, she was a very, very beautiful girl.

Rau's commanding beauty and willingness to strip down for her roles ensured her a steady career in late sixties/early seventies sex films. Although the actress tends to get overshadowed by her *Daughters of Darkness* co-stars in discussion around the film, her early years in cinema were extremely interesting when you consider the projects she worked on, and the other names involved. For example, one of her earliest major roles was in *Sexy Susan Knows How!* (1970) where Rau starred opposite Eurocult legend Rosalba Neri. The *Sexy Susan* films, which started in the late sixties, were a series of German-language sex comedies where a number of European cult actresses started out. For example, giallo queen Edwige Fenech began getting her first major roles in this arena, and did her own *Sexy Susan* film in 1968, in *Sexy Susan Sins Again*. Likewise, Rau also worked for German producer Artur Brauner, the man responsible for some of Jess Franco's signature works from the early seventies, such as *Vampyros Lesbos* (1971) — a film with its own connection to *Daughters of Darkness* which will be explored in Chapter Two — and *She Killed in Ecstasy* (1971). The actress appeared in Franco's Brauner-produced *Robinson and his Tempestuous Slaves* (1972), the year after she played Ilona in *Daughters of Darkness*. Following the success of *Daughters of Darkness* Rau continued to work steadily in Eurocult and exploitation film. In 1974 she appeared in a Spanish erotic thriller, *Lola (Beyond Eroticism)* as the main protagonist, alongside David Hemmings and Alida Valli. The plot sees Hemmings as a psychopathic child-like man, who uses his position as wealthy landlord/employer in a poverty-stricken village, to exploit a young girl (Lola, played by Rau) and force her into a violent, sadomasochistic relationship where she is tormented at his hands.

Even though Rau has very little dialogue in *Daughters of Darkness*, and she has most of the nude scenes (next to Danielle Ouimet) — including a lengthy sex scene with John Karlen's Stefan, which incidentally Kümel claims is the first scene in cinematic history to portray a male orgasm, in a realistic sense — she exudes a hypnotising presence in her role as Ilona. Kümel is particularly fond of the actress's performance in his film. When questioned about his experience working with her, his answer is enthusiastic:

> Andrea Rau, she looked great. She had a great personality and I liked her very much. I thought she was sweet and endearing. For these kind of films, one does need to have sex appeal and film personality, that mysterious ingredient nobody can define; nobody has ever been able to define. Andrea, she had it. And close-ups loved her too!

SUPPORTING CAST

Daughters of Darkness uses a small, intimate cast, much like Kümel's earlier features *Monsieur Hawarden* and *De grafbewaker*, which works well with the themes of isolation inherent in the narrative. While limited in number, there are a handful of peripheral characters who are all memorable due to the calibre of actors who played them. The director picked established theatre and film actors to play these roles in order to achieve a sense of presence for each consecutive part. For instance, Paul Esser, who plays the hotel's concierge, was not only a well-respected German actor, but a director in his own right. According to a 2011 commentary track that Kümel recorded for the film's Blu-ray release, Esser was somewhat vain, and refused to alter his hair to look like an older man, suggesting instead he would 'play grey'. Fons Rademakers, who took the part of 'Lady Chiltern', known otherwise as 'Mother', was a last-minute addition — originally any mention of Stefan's mother in the script related to just that. Kumel's decision to add in an angle of sexual ambiguity on Stefan's part lends the narrative an even more complex twist. Rademakers was the first Dutch director to be nominated for an Oscar, for his film *Village by the River* (1958). Meanwhile, *Daughters of Darkness* was the last screen role for Belgian actor Georges Jamin, who had enjoyed a career in cinema which spanned over four decades.

FILMING

Because the film was to be set in contemporary times, Kümel had some very strong ideas about how his characters should look. He modelled his two lead vampires, Bathory and Ilona, on classic stars Marlene Dietrich and Louise Brookes, respectively. When asked if it was his intention to relate his stars to the Golden era of Hollywood, Kümel replied,

> That was totally intentional. Because she [Bathory] has to represent someone immortal. The only immortal things we know in our time are cinema goddesses. Everyone knows Marlene Dietrich. Everyone knows Rita Hayworth. These people don't exist in reality, I know. But cinema is not reality, of course.

Central to the look and style of Bathory and Ilona was the costuming – exquisite gowns by Parisian designer Bernard Perris, some of which Seyrig had to be sewn into. Seyrig's sequinned dress, which she wears at the climatic dinner party, was particularly uncomfortable and heavy for the star to wear. Kümel remembers Perris and is particularly proud of the work he did for his film:

In France his name was very well known. The little black dress for Ilona was also made by him. That is one of the most difficult kinds of dresses to make: a good little black dress. I find it extremely important how you dress your people. Costumes are very important. Good actors love being dressed well, to be made up well, and to be glamourised. If you look at women in our time they look dreadful, mostly because they are awfully photographed. In most of my films the women are very well represented. I like to look at them. And it shows.

Kümel also credits his cinematographer Eduard van der Enden for capturing his stars in a glamourous light, which helped to enhance the feeling of Hollywood glamour. Van der Enden had previously worked with the director on *Monsieur Hawarden*. Kümel recalls,

> The director of photography must like a woman to make her beautiful or interesting. I worked with the very best director of photography in Britain at that time, Gerry Fisher, for *Malpertuis*. But he was not keen on making beautiful close-ups. But my dutch DOP [van der Enden], he liked it. He wasn't as good as doing atmospheric painterly cinema, certainly not, but he was fabulous at photographing women.

The production began on July 7th, 1970. Shooting during the height of summer — a very hot one at that, according to Kümel — posed some problems in regards to capturing the right mood for the piece, when you take into account that the story occurs mainly at a hotel during its off-season period. Kümel worked around this by using footage he already had of the Belgian countryside in winter, to set the initial atmosphere as the characters Stefan and Valerie arrive by train. Similarly, in a later scene where Stefan and Valerie leave Brugge — after witnessing the murder victim — further winter footage was edited in with the newly filmed action. For the rest, the crew had to make the best of what they had. Thankfully, with many of the exteriors shot at night, although impending darkness posed its own particular problems, the low light helped to mask the contrasting season.

Shooting in low light for much of the time caused its own set of frustrations. Even inside the hotel, daylight had to be eradicated wherever possible, which took a toll on the cast and crew. Danielle Ouimet reveals:

> The worst part of it was it had to be done always in darkness. Even in the daytime they were putting shades in the windows. So we would never see the day. It was very,

very rare that we would see sun. We were always in a hotel where there were no windows. If there was a room with windows, it was all blocked. For a month and a half we were totally in darkness. So it was getting on our nerves. We only had one day, on Saturdays, just to relax. And that was it. But we were working, as usual, 12 hours a day.

For Kümel, working on a strict budget, where time is always money, lighting the exterior scenes was somewhat problematic, as he explains:

It was to be shot very quickly. We had to shoot at dawn and after sunset for exteriors and that was difficult to match because we didn't have much money. And for the rest, at that time, film stock was not as supple as digital stock is now. Digital is far easier to use in terms of lighting. Back then it was called 'the magic half hour'; this moment in the day when you can shoot in low light. It was more a magic quarter of an hour actually. You had to shoot very quickly and that made problems for a small budget film.

Despite this, the director remained unfazed. For him, the art of film represents more of a practical challenge, as opposed to an artistic one:

You know, when a film is adequately directed there is never a real problem. People tend to see the film as the end result, which is normal of course. They don't realise that it is a lot of technique and very little inspiration. Film is a technical problem. The 'art' is applying solutions to express something. It's nothing more, nothing less. But it always surprises me that so few people are capable of doing it, because it is very easy. Very few people have the concentration to do that. And most people who do art play at being artists, not at being good craftspeople. It is a craft. The better craftsmen are the better filmmakers, that's all. The rest is all gobbledygook, journalistic gobbledygook. As you know journalists know nothing about everything. But they prefer to hear from directors, 'Oh I was inspired by this, or this or this'. Can you imagine that it is not like that? They lie when they say that. They lie.

The director's practical way of working with a team of actors, who were motivated from a more emotional artistic place, caused difficulties on set, especially for the less experienced performers like Ouimet. The actress found the experience somewhat stressful as a result, but fully appreciates, in retrospect, that Kümel was a very driven man, and that his behaviour was all for the common good. Speaking candidly the star says,

This guy [Kümel] he was marvellous. In retrospect I can say that he was disturbed man. But he knew exactly what to create in a film. It was a success. When you look at that film it is interesting in a way that very few people can deliver, mostly because of him. The problem with Harry is that he didn't know how to direct us exactly. I remember two scenes. The first, was when John Karlen arrived in Belgium about two days after my arrival. He [Kümel] came to my room and he said 'I want you to be in the lobby in five minutes. I do not want you to take the elevator. I want you to take the staircase that leads you to the lobby. And I want you to walk in the middle of the staircase.' Why did he want me to do this? I guess he wanted me to find this guy so beautiful, I would fall in love. It would be perfect within the film, with this kind of magic that he wanted to create. I don't know. Anyway, I did what he wanted. I found John was perfect, but I didn't fall in love immediately.

Another thing I am going to tell you that was quite weird, is about the opening scene, in the train and I am making love with my husband and the train stops. He [Kümel] had to tell us what to do, because we didn't know exactly what his plan was. It was on a real train. There was this little bunk-bed. So we were waiting for the directions he would give us. And then suddenly he takes out a book — he told me that he bought it by mail — with different positions in it. A sex book! And he says, 'OK we are going to try page two, and then this other page'. I felt weird about it. Weird, weird, weird. Because it was like, oh my God, do we have to take the same position? When I think of him, this director, I always have this same image. He was looking at this text, and he's in his bubble. He doesn't get out of it. And he's looking at the text, and he's trying to find what to tell us to do. John and I, we felt like we had to try things by ourselves and get his approval after. That's what we did actually. And we got very close because of this.

Tensions soon started to rise and the shoot, on a tight schedule and budget, was fraught with differences of opinion, which culminated in an explosive episode one day when Ouimet showed up late for a take. The director felt frustrated by what he saw as Ouimet's inexperience, which was compounded by the fact that apart from Seyrig, all the other actors were sent to him by producers. Everything finally came to a head, as the actress explains:

One day the production was very late. And that day I remember very well, because he [Kümel] was nervous because of that. I arrived on set, and again he was badgering. 'No, can't you see, you are interfering now. Go in the makeup room and I will call you.' I was putting my costume on at the last minute because he didn't want me wearing it before. When I arrived in France, he took me to every place and had me try on clothing. Days and days. Just to make sure that he knew exactly what I was going to wear. And the costume I had was a sort of a fur costume, a very thin lamb's skin costume. I noticed it was torn. I had to have it sewed for the scene. So, when he called me, I was late on the stage because of this problem. And then he comes to me, again he's saying 'Hey, you're late!' That was it! I said, 'No! Just a minute! You were with me. You were supposed to take care of this costume. You didn't do it. And I am late because of that!' And he gave me a whack! I remember I had someone trying to calm me by combing my hair with a brush. I took the brush and I just went smack! He took me by the arm, and took me in another room and said 'Not in front of my crew, if you want to tell me something. Not in front of my crew!' I said, 'That's enough Harry, you will never talk to me again like this!'. I was yelling, and everyone in the back could hear exactly what was going on. He said, 'I am going to hit you again!' I didn't wait. I just turned and jumped at him. All the furniture went on us. It was unbelievable!

So, the crew came in. They removed the furniture, and they parted us. I went to the make up room and I was crying, I was trying to not undo whatever was done. I went into the room and John was there. He was in his suit, where he was naked underneath, a bathrobe, it was red I think. And he says, 'What's the matter baby?' I said, 'Well... he hit me.' John says, 'Did you hit him first, or did he hit you first?' 'No, he hit me first. Everyone on the staff can tell you'. I remember trying to stop him, because he started running towards the set. I was trying to get him by the bathrobe. 'Don't do this! Don't do this!' He arrived on the set, he said, 'Harry'...and gave him a whack in the face. Harry fell on the floor. Oh my god! He said, 'You don't touch Danielle! You never touch a lady!'

The production was stopped and we had to call the producer in France, because there was a problem. The next day, there's silence. I remember the scene was the one where she [Seyrig] kisses me and there's a little bit of blood. She was in front of me, we were not talking. We knew exactly what we had to do. We only had to stand for the lighting to be done on our faces. She was filing her nails. I will always remember that. She's filing her nails. She's not looking at me, but I was about two feet from her, because of the test. And she says, 'Oh Harry can you come here please?' And Harry says, 'Yes Delphine'. And she says, 'I have something to tell you. When two actors — and then she pointed her nail file to her and me — are very good, you don't need a director'. She told him that right in front of me! I couldn't believe this girl. She took my part. She never told me you were right, he's badgering you, he's a bad guy. She never did that. She deliberately, in front of me, told him to run away and just do his job but we would do the rest. My god it felt good!

And after that, it went OK. I was listening much more. He was calmer. It went well I guess. I was not ready to do such a film. And maybe and I should have taken some lessons. Because the film was supposed to be done in French, actually. When we arrived, the script was in French. Then Kümel realises, the German girl [Rau] could speak English, but her French was very poor. He also realised John Karlen's accent in French was terrible, but he spoke English. Then he saw I could speak English. Delphine could also speak English because she lived there. So they changed everything and the script was then done in English. In a week it all changed completely. I had learned everything in French and then I had to translate it to English. Totally, in a week, it was very demanding.

LOCATIONS

Daughters of Darkness uses two completely separate locations, with Kümel blending them effortlessly into a single place. The interiors were mainly filmed inside The Astoria Hotel, in Brussels. The dining room and exteriors were shot in the Hotel Thermae Palace, Ostend.

Each hotel has a very different personality. The Thermae Palace, which sits on the windswept beaches of Ostend, is an imposing structure. The front is garnished with stone pillars, giving it a stately, imposing facade. The interiors were designed in art deco style. Although the hotel has changed hands over the years, and has fallen into disrepair a number of times, the stained-glass window, which adorns the dining room where Valerie and Stefan sit having their first meal at the hotel when Bathory arrives, is still intact. The hotel was initially built as a health spa, housing fresh seawater pools, a facility for natural well water, and thermal baths, which were all the rage when the building originally opened in 1933.

The Astoria, on the other hand, although less grandiose on the outside, is a far more ornate affair internally. Kümel and producer/co-writer Pierre Drouot chose the hotel because of its grand staircase, which becomes a centrepiece in the film. Many scenes show the main players either ascending from, or descending to, the hotel lobby via the Astoria's very unique staircase. The hotel dates back to slightly earlier than the Thermae Palace. It was opened in 1909, having been built on the orders of King Leopold II for the Brussels World Fair.

As well as the lobby and staircase, which both feature prominently in the film, Kümel and his crew also used apartments in the hotel, and the lounge area. One of the apartments, where the fateful scene of Ilona's death occurs, posed a particular problem because the walls were covered entirely in reflective black tiles. In order to get round this, all the crew present had to cover themselves completely in black material, with only holes cut out for their eyes, and the camera was masked in cloth also. Given the heat of the season this proved to be an uncomfortable exercise for the director and his team.

Further complications came in matching the two buildings, so that the illusion is flawless and they appear to be one and the same. The way this was achieved was by building a replica French door from the interior of the Astoria, just off the lounge room, and then installing it at the entrance of the dining room in the Thermae Palace. Likewise, at the entrance of the Thermae Palace where a revolving door is seen, a painting of the lobby in the Astoria was placed into shot, so from the outside it looks like the same building. Kümel illuminates on the art of illusion:

> That's usual in films to do that. You just you have to find an image, which matches the two locations. We used a painting, for the Ostend entrance, which had the backing of the location in Brussels. That was what made the link. Everybody believes that what see, at a certain point. Cecil B. DeMille, in the film called Reap the Wild Wind, was looking for an ending. Someone came up with the idea of using a giant squid, and Cecil B. DeMille thought that was very good. The man who proposed that to him said and make it a red squid. All the collaborators of Cecil B. DeMille said, 'Oh Cecil,

nobody will ever believe it!' And Cecil B. DeMille answered, 'Listen, when I show it them, the audience, they will believe.' That's the way cinema is made.

THE SCORE

Had his life not been cut so short, due to a diving accident at the age of 36, François de Roubaix might today be recognised as one of the greatest composers in film history. Roubaix was a completely self-taught artist, an autodidact, who successfully mastered a number of instruments entirely through obsessive self-study (from the age of 15 onwards, where he initially formed a passion for jazz, an aspect which continued to echo throughout his work), and a pioneer in the fields of both experimental music and early home studio technology. Throughout his short but sweet career, Roubaix scored films for directors such as Robert Enrico (amongst many others: *Les Grandes Gueules*, 1966; *Les aventuriers*, 1967) and Jean-Pierre Melville (*Le Samouraï*, 1967), as well as working extensively in French film and television, and educational films produced by his own father, Paul de Roubaix. The composer is also notable in the Eurocult sphere for having produced the soundtrack for Bruno Gantillon's *Girl Slaves of Morgana Le Fay* (1971), where he was credited under the name Cisco El Rubio.

Roubaix's score for *Daughters of Darkness* is a strange hybrid of Hungarian folk influences and his own unique breed of electronica. As director Kümel revealed on a commentary track for the film, the young avant-garde musician wasn't his natural choice to score the film. Instead the director felt someone like Bernard Herrmann would have been a better fit. Kümel suggested in his commentary that Herrmann may have provided something more traditionally in-keeping with the Eastern European flavours conjured by Bathory's presence.

This said, there is no denying that Roubaix's music for the film, especially the signature track 'Les Dunes D'ostende', is part of what gives *Daughters of Darkness* such a haunting atmosphere. Roubaix, like French director Jean Rollin, was born in Neuilly-sur-Seine, a commune to the West of Paris. Interestingly, both the composer and the cult filmmaker had their own obsessions with the ocean and coast. For Rollin, windswept beaches became a key poetic motif in his most memorable films. With Roubaix, his obsession with the sea played a slightly less prominent role in his work overall, although it is still there to find, especially in the more fluid and free jazz elements he often employed in his music. However, Roubaix's love for diving — ironically the activity that ended his life — was as important to him as making music. For him, the two worlds were inseparable. It is perhaps because of this that Roubaix's affinity to the sea shines through in his soundtrack to *Daughters of Darkness*, a film set entirely on the coast, more so than in many of his other film scores. The composer captures the poetry found in the loneliness of deserted beaches — just as Rollin did in the images he created from this particular inspiration — thus lending the film an eerie quality that only supports the offbeat performances and striking imagery at play.

FOOTNOTES

1. The actress also starred in *Accident* (1967), directed by Joseph Losey, with a screenplay adapted by Pinter from a novel by Nicholas Mosley

Chapter Two: Vampyros Lesbos

Daughters of Darkness was just one of many vampire films to surface in 1971 and one of a number from that period classed as 'lesbian' vampire films in one way or another. Very few of these films were made with a focus on the Bathory myth specifically — the handful of films that did will be explored in the next chapter. The rise in popularity of vampire erotica, flavoured with Sapphic notes, was partly due to the success of Hammer Studios' *The Vampire Lovers*, made the year before in 1970. Prior to this period, female vampires were vastly overshadowed by their male counterparts in cinema. If we consider the two seminal texts in vampire literature, J. Sheridan Le Fanu's *Carmilla* (published 1872), and Bram Stoker's *Dracula* (1897), and then look at how many times each has been adapted for film, it becomes clear that cinematic vampirism, at least traditionally, has largely taken place inside a male-dominated arena, with filmic versions of *Dracula* outnumbering *Carmilla* at least tenfold. That is not to say there were no female vampires in cinema up until 1970, but, for the ones that did exist, the emphasis often centred on male power and domination.

This was especially the case for Christopher Lee's various incarnations of Dracula. Lee starred in Hammer's original Dracula film, *Dracula* (1958), and then a further seven sequels. What became noteworthy was the fact that the actor did something quite remarkable in sexualising the character, given that during most of his performances he barely uttered a word of dialogue, which then set a precedent for others to follow. For Barry Forshaw,

> ... the Hammer version of Dracula, in which the vampiric Count is not presented as the straightforwardly monstrous creature of the Browning Bela Lugosi version, but (in Christopher Lee's mesmeric interpretation) as an elegant, dangerously attractive and cultivated figure with immense erotic appeal. However little his character is inclined to (or, for that matter, able to — who knows?) indulge in straightforward sexual activity, there is a metaphor for sexual threat implied, with a libidinous charge more insidious than any more conventional erotic presentation would be. (Forshaw 2013: xx)

It would take some twelve years following the release of *Dracula* for a female to rival the sexual potency and dominating characteristics of Lee's vampire to arrive on screen.

Ingrid Pitt, in the role of Mircalla/Carmilla Karnstein for *The Vampire Lovers* played the part as a sexual predator in line with the original text. While there had been hints of this in previous films, nothing compared to the unrestrained screen presence of Pitt. The actress is quoted as saying that she wanted to become a female counterpart to Christopher Lee's male sexualised vampire, outlining in a 1998 Sy-Fy Channel interview that women 'only get remembered as horror queens when they play predators, not victims'. This was certainly the case for Barbara Steele whose face dominated Italian Gothic horror throughout the 1960s because of her association with the evil predatory vampiric witch, Asa Vajda, in Mario Bava's *Black Sunday* (1960). *Black Sunday* effectively laid down the blueprint from which a decade-long cycle of Gothic features would evolve, films that were far more gruesome and sexually perverse than their British and American counterparts. At the time it was produced it was relatively unheard of to have a woman playing the main villain in a horror film. And yet, this was obviously something audiences were craving, because as a result of the success of her memorable performance in Bava's film, British actress Barbara Steele was able to carve out a niche for herself in further like-minded Italian Gothics. She is now ranked as one of the few women considered true classic horror icons, alongside her male contemporaries, Peter Cushing, Christopher Lee, Vincent Price and Boris Karloff.

Just a year later Hammer would go on to produce two other films in the same vein, *Lust for a Vampire* (1971) and *Twins of Evil* (1971). Although the associated plots digressed from Le Fanu's original story somewhat, the three films would form what was unofficially dubbed The Karnstein Trilogy — with a fourth loose sequel *Captain Kronos: Vampire Hunter* (1974) added later on.

While Pitt's performance in *The Vampire Lovers* set the bar, which arguably remained unrivalled by the other episodes in the Hammer Karnstein saga, it would take Delphine Seyrig's Bathory to top it. Cold, calculating, sadistic, the Countess Bathory of *Daughters of Darkness* is a female vampire like no other. The brilliance of *Daughters of Darkness* lies in the way it plays with Gothic tradition, embraces the essence of French Fantastique (which we will discuss at greater length later), and the fact it takes advantage of the erotic film market and loosening of censorship, to not only thrill audiences, but provide them with a film that delivers substance and subtext by the bucketload. As a lesbian vampire film, above all other things, it has a direct connection to literary tradition — to be explored elsewhere in this book — as well as to an entire canon of lesbian vampire cinema, which developed from the early 1930s up until the 1970s. This chapter will examine some of those cinematic connections, to see where the film fits with its peers and contemporaries.

CLASSIC CINEMA AND THE CARMILLA CONNECTION

While it is true that Le Fanu's *Carmilla* was largely ignored by cinema, until lesbianism became an acceptable subject matter in the 1970s, one of the most influential vampire pictures of all time, Carl Theodor Dreyer's *Vampyr* (1932), credited Le Fanu's *In A Glass Darkly* — the collection in which *Carmilla* was first published — as the basis for the underlying screenplay. However, Dreyer's interpretation of the text bears little resemblance to the writer's work, and even less to anything traditionally thought of as a 'classic vampire film'. The only obvious connection appears to be in the main vampire's ability to penetrate the minds of young women, and hold them under a spell. Just like in the original novella the central vampire, Carmilla, can invade the dreams of her victims, as if haunting them with a form of psychic attack.

Although Dreyer's work is widely credited as having an influence on countless later vampire films, including *Daughters of Darkness* — where it was referenced in the original press book to accompany the theatrical release — Dreyer's narrative remains original and unimitated. It would appear that while many filmmakers have taken the lead from the director in regards to mood, lighting, shadows and other technical aspects, and even though his dreamlike, fantastical way of telling the story has inspired countless others, the central story, which involves an old hag as vampire, no fangs, no claws, crosses or garlic or other ephemera, and certainly no blood, did not really catch on. Until *Daughters of Darkness* that is, which doesn't revel in any of the usual trademarks of vampirism in an overt sense, just like Dreyer's film. When asked if she knew, during the production, just how unique *Daughters of Darkness* was, compared to the rest of the vampire cinema coming out at the time, actress Danielle Ouimet replied,

> We could see it was different from the fact that we had no teeth growing, we had no garlic around us. Like when Stefan dies because his wrist is slashed. Well, he's not a

vampire. This is for real. The vampire at the end, she dies because she is impaled. This is not a usual take on how we think about vampires. When you think of vampires you think of garlic, you think of growing teeth, you think of blood. Anyway, I call it 'vampire psychologique', a psychological vampire film. It was more of a weird story than a vampire film for me.

Camille Paglia also noted how tonally different *Daughters of Darkness* was compared to its peers, placing it in the psychological bracket when she wrote about it in *Sexual Personae* (1990):

Violent horror films, of the splattering kind now so common, seem to me a most pedestrian taste. A classy genre of vampire films follows a style I call Psychological High Gothic. It begins in Coleridge's medieval *Christabel* and its descendents, Poe's *Ligeia* and James' *Turn of the Screw*. A good example is *Daughters of Darkness* (1971), starring Delphine Seyrig as an elegant lesbian vampire. High Gothic is abstract and ceremonious. Evil has become world-weary, hierarchical glamour. There is no bestiality. The theme is eroticized western power, the burden of history. *The Hunger* (1983) comes close to being a masterpiece of this genre but is ruined by horrendous errors, as when the regal Catherine Deneuve is made to crawl around on all fours, slavering over cut throats. Please. Butchery is not the point of vampirism. Sex — domination and submission — is. Gothic horror must be moderated by Apollonian discipline, or it turns into gross buffoonery. The run-of-the-mill horror film is anti-aesthetic and anti-idealizing. Its theme sparagmos, the form of pulverising energies of Dionysus. Horror films unleash the forces repressed by Christianity — evil and barbarism of nature. (1990: 268)

Where Dreyer's *Vampyr* is also pertinent to *Daughters of Darkness* is in its use of a matriarch figure as all-powerful and dangerous. While an old lady who sleeps in a coffin might not seem particularly threatening, the fact she can exert mind control over her victims, and other villagers, makes her something of a force to be reckoned with. As Pam Keesey suggests, 'the old woman, Carmilla, more closely resembles the witches of classic fairy tales' (1997: 96). As we will see later, the fairy tale, and its associated genres, especially the fantastique, play a big role in the universe of *Daughters of Darkness*. Keesey's observation is an interesting one, given that witches are often placed in folklore not just as figures of evil, but wise women. In neo pagan wicca the Crone, the last cycle of life, the archetype of the witch – haggard, old, ugly – is also associated with knowledge and the power that knowledge brings. Therefore, in using this combination of age and wisdom, the female vampire may not be as physically powerful as her male counterpart, but she is able to dominate purely through mental strength.

Bathory, as depicted by Delphine Seyrig, is the opposite of the crone-like woman who appears in Vampyr. This aside, the Countess, just as the hag, also carries the wisdom that comes with age and is highly attuned to the fickle nature of humanity, as well as all its weaknesses. She studies her victims prior to going in for attack, plays with them, rarely having to resort to physical violence, unless it is to feed; the latter aspect is something the director keeps off-camera for the most part. Kümel stops short at having Bathory be able to get into the minds of her victims in any concrete way, unlike some of the adaptations of *Carmilla* — especially *Blood and Roses* (1960) or *The Velvet Vampire* (1971) — however, it is through the use of psychological warfare the Countess becomes an unstoppable force, even for the most strong-willed of characters like Stefan.

After *Vamyr*, *Carmilla* would not be adapted again until the 1960s. However, there is one other female vampire, another rare example from this early period, who shares some distinct traits with the vampire women of *Daughters of Darkness*: *Dracula's Daughter*. In 1936, Universal followed up their highly successful *Dracula*, with the female-fronted sequel, for which screenwriter John Balderston wrote the initial treatment using Bram Stoker's short story 'Dracula's Guest' as a model. As highlighted by Jon Towlson, 'While Balderston's treatment reprised the basic plot for *Dracula* the intended *frisson* of the proposed sequel essentially came out of portraying Szekely [the female vampire central to the plot] as a dominatrix' (2016: 312).

Two years previously, in 1934, the Motion Picture Producers and Distributors of America, brought into force the Production Code — known more widely as the Hays Code — which enforced moral boundaries on any films made within its system. Within this scope, depictions of topics such as homosexuality, premarital sex, sadomasochism and lesbianism were strictly prohibited. *Dracula's Daughter* is a perfect example of how filmmakers tested the limitations of the code in its early days. Directors working in the domain of horror film had previously enjoyed freedom to add in subversion and transgression more or less as they pleased, to provide audiences with the thrill they craved. Suddenly they found themselves in a strange no man's land where the tastiest subject matter was off the menu. Writers and filmmakers had to get clever if they wanted to get around the rules.

Balderston's original idea for *Dracula's Daughter* attempted to test the code's limits, which was still very much in its infancy at this point. As Towlson continues:

> As long as it was done by suggestion, Balderston argued, the censors would allow this element of sadomasochism in the film and it would be justified dramatically by the fact that the female vampire needs blood, 'but can get it in other ways than merely biting their necks': 'I want to see for instance her loathsome, deaf-mute servants carry into her boudoir… savage looking whips, chains, straps, etc., and hear the cries of her victims without ever seeing exactly what happens. We had none of this sort of thing in the original DRACULA. I feel sure that so long as it is a women torturing men the thing is not too unendurable, as it would have been had Dracula so treated his female victims.' (2016: 310)

Balderston's treatment was never realised. The eventual script took on a completely different form. Instead *Dracula's Daughter* revolved around the story of Countess Marya Zaleska (renamed from Szekely, and played by Gloria Holden), Count Dracula's cursed daughter, who embarks on stealing her father's body from the morgue following his destruction, with a hope of setting herself free and become mortal so she may live a normal life. That's not to say the film does not attempt to dip its toe into the pool of transgression. The Countess still needs to feed, and does so from both male and female victims. There is one particularly daring scene, for the time, where the vampire lures a young woman (portrayed by Nan Grey) to her townhouse, on the ruse she is a painter and wants a model. The girl is asked to strip (we get to see the victim uncover her shoulder) before Zaleska moves in for the kill. The piece is loaded with lesbian notes, even if director Lambert Hillyer was careful not to show anything too graphic.

Where *Dracula's Daughter* connects to *Daughters of Darkness*, beyond the obvious 'Daughter' connection in the title, is in two decidedly different strains of thought. First off, we have the dominatrix theme, which came from *Dracula's Daughter*'s original treatment. This may have been a step too far in 1936, but by 1971 directors were ready for it.

Or at least Harry Kümel was, in a fashion. While Kümel might not have been prepared to show his Countess loaded up with whips and chains, he uses lurid conversation to hammer home the point she is a sadist through and through. The audience doesn't need to see what goes on in her private torture chamber, they feel it through the dialogue, as she explores the sadomasochistic side of the Bathory legend in a scene that takes place between the Countess, Stefan and Valerie:

Valerie: Imagine, she [Countess Bathory] bled 300 virgins to death.

Bathory: Some say 800, a woman will do anything to stay young.

Valerie: Drinking human blood?!

Sefan: She believed human blood was the elixir of youth.

Bathory: Exactly. Do you know of her?

Stefan: Yes, I've read about her. She kidnapped young girls and kept them chained to give blood. Blood for her to bathe in and drink.

Valerie: [exclaiming in disgust] No!!

Bathory: [getting enjoyment from Valerie's discomfort] Oh, yes, yes!

Stefan: And she hung them up by the wrists and then whipped them until their tortured flesh was torn to shreds.

Bathory: Yes, that's it. And she clipped off their fingers with shears.

Valerie: No!

Stefan: She pricked their bodies with needles.

Bathory: Yes, she tore out their nipples with silver pincers.

Stefan: She bit them everywhere.

Valerie: No!

Stefan: And then she pushed white hot pokers into their faces and when they parted their lips to scream she shoved the flaming sword up into their mouths.

Bathory: [visually excited by this point] Oh yes, go on, go on!

Stefan: She pierced their veins with rusty nails, slit their throats.

Bathory: So that their young bodies pumped out young blood over her naked skin. Blood, beautiful red blood. Her hands, and her arms, and legs and her face.

Valerie: Stop it! Both of you!

The visuals evoked by the dialogue in this particular scene are horrific, made even more gruesome by the fact that Bathory and Stefan are both visually aroused in recounting all the gory details. The tension is suffocating. Even though nothing is actually happening, Valerie's sensitivity towards the matter, the way she squirms in her chair, becoming more and more distressed, is extremely effective in letting the audience know just how cruel the Countess is. Prior to this, it is intimated that Ilona is in love with her master, Bathory, but also terribly afraid. Yet, Kümel is careful to avoid letting viewers know what is behind this fear in any concrete terms. Ilona wants to leave, but can't. Bathory has made her into a complete submissive. In this one single dialogue scene, where Bathory's past is explored by the Countess and Stefan, everything is suddenly made clear. The director doesn't need one drop of blood, or a glimpse of leather or chains, to make his point.

Ilona's case brings us to the second link to *Dracula's Daughter*: the idea of immortality as a curse, and therefore something painful to bear. Gloria Holden's portrayal of Countess Marya Zaleska is a haunting one, romantic in its emotional layers; where sentiment such as loneliness and longing are central to the plot. Zaleska yearns to be free, just as Ilona does. By contrast, Countess Bathory is a libertine through and through. She has no qualms about living for eternity, as long as she can continue to enjoy her sadistic games, and the pleasure of feasting on flesh. Her associate is tired of this life. We see the girl doesn't share the same sentiment, attempting to leave, thinking now that Bathory has a new toy, in the form of Valerie and Stefan, she might be granted permission to slip away. This isn't the case. You certainly get the idea no-one is allowed to leave Countess Bathory, not alive at least. Zaleska suffers a similar pain. Her love for a mortal man, her longing for a human life, overshadows the more horrific elements in the film. Ultimately, *Dracula's Daughter* becomes a lament on wanting things you cannot have, and the suffering that brings. Ilona's plight follows a similar arc.

Dracula's Daughter set a trend that other female vampires would follow. In the case of their male counterparts, sexual aggression and domination ruled. For the women, vampirism was often set out as accidental, a curse, and as a result was framed as something which impacts on mental state and causes neurotic behaviour. Although earlier films used this line of thinking in subtle ways, especially to explain away female monstrosity not as a source of power, but as a weakness, the aforementioned performance of Ingrid Pitt in *The Vampire Lovers* combined both aspects of male and female: sexual predator and cursed romantic. Pitt's role in that film, although horribly monstrous, also comes loaded with much pathos. Her obsession with her victim, Emma Morton (played by Madeline Smith) is one of suffocation, coupled with a desire to be loved by the girl. Although Kümel does not employ this with Bathory, for she is a cruel, cold character — her wish to be loved and adored appears to stem from extreme narcissism as opposed to any real emotion — he does use the curse angle through the character of Ilona to great effect. In essence he is able to achieve the best of both worlds through the two separate characters.

DAUGHTERS OF DARKNESS AND THE FRENCH FANTASTIQUE

When asked if *Daughters of Darkness*, or at least a film like it, could be made today Harry Kümel is cynical. For Kümel, films should not portray realism, rather they should capture dream worlds, provide the means for escapism in order to give respite from the humdrum of everyday life. He explains:

> It is the idiotic imbecile opinion of film critics who like to say that films are like life. You hear all these bejeweled people in Cannes applauding films about workers. You hear them, jewels clinking, but at the same time they applaud that kind of film because it gives them a good conscience. That's the reason why all these actors and entertainers like to pose as socially conscious. And that is not my kind of cup of tea. That's why we need films that are like fairy tales. People need fairy tales. Now the fairy tales are nightmares. We no longer have things where people come out of the cinema with a good feeling. Because giving good feelings to people is considered politically incorrect.

Whether Kümel's sentiment is entirely true, the director does have a point to some degree. People *do* need fairy tales, they always have, and this is why so many classic stories of this type have survived, being told and retold over centuries.

Daughters of Darkness might not immediately strike people as a fairy tale. It differs from traditional folk stories in that it doesn't come with the moral message most of them were designed to give. Our 'Princess' Valerie doesn't get her prince. There is no romance in a traditional sense. And good definitely doesn't triumph over evil. What needs to be considered in some depth is the special connection *Daughters of Darkness* has with one of the fairy tale's cinematic offspring, the fantastique or fantastic; a genre which stemmed from popular folk-based storytelling, as it branched off into the realm of the unexplainable and mysterious, and was mixed up with aspects of Gothic and even (as we will see in the next chapter) French symbolism. It is worth noting that all of these genres — the fairy tale, the folk tale, Gothic, symbolism, and the fantastique — are interconnected; often serving a similar purpose, and holding the same space within our imaginations. As Jason Marc Harris explains:

> ...the Gothic and other literary traditions of fantasy and the fantastic have extended and stylized motifs and metaphysicals that were long standing in folklore to begin with. Margaret Carter in *Specter or Delusions The Supernatural in Gothic Fiction* reminds us that the term Gothic originates 'from the eighteenth century ... to describe the Middle Ages, especially in their barbaric and superstitious aspects'. (2008: 19)

The fantastique, and its tradition in cinema, is a nebulous term that many struggle to define. The way in which it differs from Gothic, and indeed the fairy tale, is its ambiguous nature. As Todorov explains:

> Which brings us to the very heart of the fantastic. In a world which is indeed our world, the one we know, a world without devils, sylphides, or vampires, there occurs an event which cannot be explained by the laws of this same familiar world. The person who experiences the event must opt for one of two possible solutions: either he is a victim of an illusion of the senses, of a product of the imagination — the laws of the world then remain what they are; or else the event has indeed taken place, it is an integral part of reality — but then this reality is controlled by laws unknown to us. [...] The fantastic occupies the duration of this uncertainty. Once we choose one answer or the other, we leave the fantastic for a neighbouring genre, the uncanny or the marvellous. The fantastic is that hesitation experienced by a person who knows

only the laws of nature confronting an apparently supernatural event. (2018: 25)

Daughters of Darkness is all about hesitation, right up until the end. Kümel refuses to dish out definitive answers and keeps all the usual vampiric tropes firmly at bay. There are no gnashing fangs. Any violence that occurs does so in a very ordinary way. The accidental killing of Ilona when she is impaled in the bathroom is one such case in point. We know she fears water. This triggers her hysteria, which then leads to the ghastly event. But water doesn't burn her skin like it does for others throughout cinematic tradition. By contrast, consider Hammer's *Dracula A.D. 1972* (1972), where we see a very graphic vampire demise by running water, or even *Dracula: Prince of Darkness* (1966), where Dracula slips under ice into a watery grave. By contrast Kümel chooses to deny viewers a reasonable explanation for Ilona's behaviour when she is confronted with the running water in the shower. He allows us to fill in the gaps with what we *think* we know about vampire lore, but never makes it clear whether this is the truth within the diegesis. Similarly, Stefan is killed with brute force and the use of a makeshift weapon in the form of a crystal bowl. Although we see the two women apparently drink his blood in the aftermath, he isn't murdered in the traditional vampiric fashion of biting or bloodsucking. Instead, Kümel conjures violence in a primal human way. It is brutal, but pedestrian and explicable.

Kümel takes the same approach in regards to Bathory's origin. The concierge is adamant he has met the woman forty years previously. He recognises her instantly. Her explanation, when confronted, is that the idea is preposterous. The reason she offers is that it must have been her mother he encountered. That doesn't stop him doubting her explanation and he even goes so far as to try and warn Stefan and Valerie. The point is hammered home, and it becomes apparent we have stepped into the realm of the fantastic. We see the concierge is perplexed by the situation. But there is some part of his mind that searches for a reasonable explanation.

Meanwhile, the retired police officer who arrives at the hotel appears to have reached the same conclusion as the concierge, as he reveals he could never forget meeting Bathory many years before. He reacquaints himself with the Countess in stating, 'those Bruge murders are somewhat special, one might say classic, the kind of thing you read about in Medieval manuscripts, you know, silly things about ghosts chased away by garlic, and vampires shrinking from crosses'. Bathory seems appalled and uncomfortable. Yet again, Kümel toys with the audience and refuses to make things concrete, instead leaving everything hanging between the lines, unspoken and merely hinted at — at one point the cop thinks he catches a glimpse that Bathory has no reflection in her compact mirror, although it could also be a trick of the angle. It is this recurrent playing, especially in the loaded dialogue, which keeps the narrative rooted in the fantastique. When asked how she stays so young, Bathory replies, with a wry smile, 'it's very simple, a very strict diet, lots of sleep'. In this, Kümel, while not spelling it out, keeps the audience in on the joke the main characters are not privy to. This nudge-nudge, wink-wink engagement with viewers ensures they are kept complicit with Bathory, and the sick joke which is currently unfolding before their very eyes.

It is through the relationship *Daughters of Darkness* has with the fantastic that it harbours a distinct connection to a much earlier film: Roger Vadim's *Blood and Roses*. The film follows a similar subtle track when it comes to spelling things out. The film uses Le Fanu's *Carmilla* as an inspiration for the script, but places events in a contemporary setting and makes some notable changes in the structure of the main plot and central characters. Annette Vadim plays Carmilla Karnstein, one of the last in the line of the Karnstein family; an ancient lineage who were once rumoured to be vampires. Apparently the last of this line was staked by villagers in 1775, although local lore continues to recount the scars of the supposed trauma, and residents of the community remain highly superstitious. Carmilla is very much human, however, as is her cousin Leopoldo (Mel Ferrer) with whom the woman has an intense infatuation. The story plays out through a love triangle between Carmilla, Leopoldo and Leopoldo's fiancee, Georgia (Elsa Martinelli), as Carmilla, eaten up by jealousy, attempts to drive a wedge between the couple by seducing them both.

Although there are two different prints in circulation of *Blood and Roses*, American and French versions, with each being slightly different,[2] the basic story is thus: jealous woman stumbles into family tomb during an engagement party, young girls start to show up dead shortly afterwards. It is suggested Carmilla is either possessed by a vampire, or just completely mad. Director Vadim, just like Harry Kümel, is careful to keep as much hidden between the lines as possible.

The fantastic element of Vadim's film is kept in place by constant rationalising at key moments of the plot. Carmilla's condition, as explained by her doctor, is a form of neurosis brought on by jealousy. When Carmilla staggers into the family crypt, during Georgia and Leopoldo's engagement party, and finds that fireworks have detonated a bomb buried there during the war, it is indicated that the spirit of her ancestor, Mircalla, works its way inside of her, and this is why she is then compelled to kill young women on the family estate. Or at least, this is what Carmilla believes has happened, or even wishes would happen — she is wearing her ancestor's wedding dress at the time the supposed possession occurs. The event then drives her to seduce her cousin and his future wife, as the woman becomes more predatory and sexually aggressive. During the foundation scenes we see a similar moment play out between the trio of Carmilla, Georgia and Leopoldo, whereby Carmilla recounts the family history, which appears to have had some influence on the aforementioned scene in *Daughters of Darkness*, as Bathory's gruesome acts are re-lived through dialogue. However, in the case of *Blood and Roses*, Georgia is not visibly distressed, and takes the conversation in good spirits.

> Carmilla: No, we are speaking about real vampires, the undead who drink the blood of the living.
>
> Leopoldo: Carmilla is right. When you open a vampire's grave, his body is intact. It's slight breathing raises his chest. A lukewarm blood is flowing in his veins. He is identical to the living, expect in his cruelty.
>
> Georgia: [unfazed] I love dark tales!

With Carmilla taken in by folk tales and superstition it is easy to believe her behaviour could just be down to her imagination. Driven to the brink by sexual frustration, one could read the film as a verse on female hysteria caused by unrequited love and the lust triggered by it. Vadim is careful to push the fantastic angle delicately, by adding in clues here and there, and suggesting all is not how it seems. It is only at the very end that we get some kind of closure, even if it's still not as concrete as many would like. The fantastic aspect is also cemented by the story's connection to fairy tales. At certain moments in the narrative, young children are seen whispering about vampires. The aesthetic of the film makes use of the pastoral settings to evoke a magical fairy tale feel during key set pieces. And then we have the villagers to consider, those who live in fear of the return of the Karnsteins as vampires, and fully believe the stories to be true. If Carmilla is driven by imagination, it is a shared belief founded on years of tales told round the fire late at night, through the nursery rhymes of young children, or terrified whispers. It is the shared consciousness that keeps alive the Karnstein story as a fantastic one, even though Leopoldo, Georgia and Carmilla's doctor search for reasonable answers to undermine local belief in the supernatural.

Ultimately *Blood and Roses* is a tale of obsession, which employs psychology over graphic violence in order to create an unsettling plot. It is here that the film bears closest comparison with *Daughters of Darkness*. In Carmilla's role as a third wheel in the relationship between Leopoldo and Georgia, she pushes them apart at any given opportunity, just like Bathory does with Valerie and Stefan. Even though Carmilla's initial interest appears to be with her cousin, as the story develops the focus of her attention shifts to Georgia. This culminates in a same-sex kiss — shocking for the time — in another of the film's key scenes that appears to have been replicated in part by Kümel later on. Carmilla's infatuation with the pair of lovers is as suffocating as Bathory's; however, given the time and place the film was made, cruelty is kept to a minimum. It is still there, kept between the lines, with both films drawing the same conclusions to explain the vampire's motivation in the film's parting shot.

The vampire film is perfect for fantastic settings, given the scope to add in mythological and fantasy elements. Much of the appeal to be found in vampires is not knowing where they came from, and mystery is often a large part of their allure. Other filmmakers who have taken advantage of this aspect include Dreyer, in his sublime use of an extended dream sequence in *Vampyr* — where the protagonist sees or imagines himself dead; something replicated in *Blood and Roses*. Similarly, French filmmaker Jean Rollin revelled in the genre, creating fantastical, otherworldly cinematic poetry from vampire stories, which outwardly appeared to have no rhyme or reason. Although the respective filmmakers, including Vadim and Kümel, interpret the fantastic in very different ways, one thing that is clear is that the tradition appears to be a very European one.

THE RISE OF THE EROTIC FEMALE VAMPIRE: REINTERPRETING GOTHIC FOR THE '60S AND '70S

1960, the year of *Blood and Roses*, was a landmark year for the genre. As the Hays Code in the United States started to weaken — it would be abolished by 1968 — and the age of permissiveness dawned all over Europe and America, the loosening of censorship allowed horror film to take on more violent and sexual subjects. It was the year that saw the release of Alfred Hitchcock's *Psycho*, a seminal film, not just for the horror genre, but for the way it tested the boundaries of censorship. Mario Bava's *Black Sunday* paved the way for the lurid sexualised Gothic horror of Italy. In France, Georges Franju's *Eyes Without a Face* mixed traditional Gothic drama with graphic scenes of facial surgery, as well as a sense of the fantastique, and poetic ambiguity. In Britain, Michael Powell's *Peeping Tom* included one of the first instances, albeit brief, of nudity in British film.

Despite this, it would take a full decade after *Blood and Rose*'s lesbian kiss for erotic vampire cinema to really come into its own. The early to mid sixties saw almost no action in breaking down heteronormative rules in the sub genre, apart from Camillo Mastrocinque's *Crypt of the Vampire* (1964) — another film inspired by *Carmilla* — which flirted with the idea of same-sex relationships, as dictated by Le Fanu's story, but was careful not to show things in any explicit detail — beyond one moment where a young girl is lured into the bedroom of another, and the door closes behind them.

Jean Rollin's *The Rape of the Vampire* (*Le Viol du Vampire*, 1968) stands out as a markedly different example amongst the rest of late sixties horror cinema, as a film that deliberately broke convention. Rollin made several films about vampires, each one very different to others. Where they are tied is in their distinct focus on female sexuality and the power it holds. It is for his emphasis on vampire queens, goddesses and Dionysian cannibal ladies that Rollin becomes most pertinent to our discussion of *Daughters of Darkness*.

The Rape of the Vampire was originally conceived as a short, but then later had a second half added, *The Vampire Woman/Queen of the Vampires*, to make a story of two halves with a running time long enough to qualify as a full-length feature. Its incoherence, due to the fragmented narrative structure, makes perfect sense when you take the film as a chapter in Rollin's body of work as a complete whole. When it came to his vampire films, Rollin favoured aspects of French symbolism, as well as surrealism and dream logic, over conventional narrative structure. The film introduces a vampire queen during its second act, which is something that had never been seen before in horror cinema up until that point. Therefore, *The Rape of the Vampire* stands as something of a game changer, even though very few other filmmakers picked up the baton it so daringly extended.

Rollin's inclusion of the Vampire Queen (played by Jacqueline Sieger) as majestic head of her coven — the gang ride around in a convertible with the top down, defying the rays of the sun — was a direct subversion of cinematic tradition. The Queen is a potent figure, and even though she enjoys very little screen time, it could be argued her cold, callous attitude, authoritative tone, and ability to command not just one or two but an entire group of vampires, makes her more of a direct descendent of Kümel's Bathory than any of the other examples cited in this chapter so far. Even Pitt's performance as Carmilla Karnstein is delivered with some sentimentality, an aspect lacking in both Rollin's Vampire Queen and the Countess of *Daughters of Darkness*. Adding to this, *The Rape of the Vampire* harnesses aspects of sadism — shown graphically in a scene where a girl is whipped, and another (blind) girl is tricked and tormented on a beach by a crowd of sadistic vampires. These same elements can also be found in *Daughters of Darkness* — although, as previously discussed, in far less graphic terms — in that each film frames the head vampire as someone who enjoys cruel games and toying with their prey.

Rollin continued to spotlight female vampires throughout his career. Not all of them were queens, but each was powerful in their own way. The director's *Shiver of the Vampires* (*Le Frisson des Vampires*, 1971), although far more fantasy based than Kümel's film, is something of a kindred spirit, in that it spotlights a couple of newlyweds, Isle and Antoine, who have their relationship pulled apart by a strong female vampire. The head vampire this time is Isolde, an ancient being with a penchant for young women, who is just as suffocating as Bathory, although her methods are not as cruel. The story depicts Isolde focusing more on seduction rather than aggression to get what she wants.

As well as seeing the release of *Daughters of Darkness* and *Shiver of the Vampires*, 1971 was a peak year for lesbian vampire films. As previously stated, Hammer set about producing a couple of sequels to *The Vampire Lovers*, *Lust for a Vampire* and *Twins of Evil*.

However, by this point they had backtracked slightly on their new daring formula and were retreating to type. Therefore, even though *Lust for a Vampire* takes place inside an all-girls school, the potential to exploit Sapphic desire from nubile young women clad in diaphanous gowns was whittled down a few minor scenes, as the focus shifted to a traditional hetreosexual relationship when the lead vampire, another incarnation of Carmilla Karnstein (played by Yutte Stensgaard), falls in love with a mortal man. By the time the studio made it to the third film in the series, *Twins of Evil*, later that year, lesbianism was relegated to suggestion and a split second of breast biting. Not that this mattered, given the strength of the previously mentioned films, and others like it flying the flag for lesbian vampires, some of which shared a distinct kinship with *Daughters of Darkness*, including *Let's Scare Jessica to Death*, *The Blood Spattered Bride*, Jess Franco's *Vampyros Lesbos* and Stephanie Rothman's *The Velvet Vampire*.

Prolific maverick, and by this point mainstay on the Eurocult circuit, Jess Franco had previously dabbled in vampiric themes with *Succubus* (1968) — a film, while not strictly a vampire film, is one which linked aspects of sex and death, albeit it in a more surreal way — and his more traditional take on the Dracula myth, *Count Dracula* (1970), which is a film that the star, Christopher Lee, seemed particularly proud of. Speaking in his first autobiography *Tall, Dark and Gruesome* (1977) Lee explained:

> My feelings about Bram Stoker's character never radically altered through seven films. Simply, it was aesthetically depressing to see the films step by step deteriorate, chiefly because after the verve and dash of their first decade, Hammer became complacent and careless, backed unimaginative scripts and tawdry production in the dangerously casual view they had a captive audience who would take anything. [...] *Count Dracula*, made against the grain of this decline by Jess Franco in Spain outside of the Hammer aegis, was a damn good try at doing the character as Bram Stoker meant him to be. In the whole vast Dracula industry it was unique in that. (1977: 262)

Franco wasn't happy to just stop there. A year later, and with one of the shining stars of *Count Dracula* film, his muse, Soledad Miranda (who had taken the part of Mina Harker), the filmmaker took Bram Stoker's core story and completely turned it on its head for *Vampyros Lesbos*. The film doesn't just incorporate aspects of Bram Stoker's tale, but also dips its toe into the Bathory legend by using a Hungarian countess, Nadine Carody

(Miranda), as well as bringing in parts of the *Carmilla* story. The result traces the plight of a female Dracula figure, who sunbathes in a white bikini beside the swimming pool, in her light and airy Turkish villa, and dances in a strip club at night. Matters take a dark turn when the countess becomes obsessed with a young woman, Linda (Ewa Strömberg) and sets about seducing her in order to turn her into a vampire. The Linda character is particularly interesting in that she appears to be an amalgamation of Stoker's characters Jonathan and Mina Harker. She meets the countess because she is sent to the island to deliver some paperwork, like Jonathan in the book, but is then pursued (as is Mina) by the count (or countess in this version). Linda's dreams are also invaded by by Carody and it is suggested that Linda's travel to the location has been predestined or somehow influenced by the vampire.

Miranda — who died in a tragic car accident aged only 27, the year before *Vampyros Lesbos* saw its official release — displays some of the same cruel and authoritative characteristics of Seyrig as Countess Bathory. However, given the stylistic contrast between the pictures, and the fact they are tonally different in many respects, it could be argued that Carody makes for a far more sensual predator than Bathory. *Daughters of Darkness* is not without its own sensual moments, it's just they don't go as far as Jess Franco's vision, with its softcore girl-on-girl action. Instead, Kümel depicts the relationship between Bathory and the women in her life — Ilona and Valerie — on more delicate terms. Bathory's intimacy with the girls is shown through caresses, little touches on the hands and face, and gentle kisses. It is all the claw behind the glove, of course. One can only imagine the great cruelty the creature is capable of, which is hinted at through blink-and-you'll-miss-them scowls and curled lips. This is all testament to Seyrig's incredibly nuanced performance, played out through gestures, pauses and a steaming hot chemistry with her co-stars. Miranda holds her own presence too, as Countess Carody, however hers is slightly different, and pivots on a sexual intensity, rather than Seyrig's suffocating cruelty. Differences aside, both films are prime examples of female potency and strength, and kick back at the previous couple of decades, where most of the female characters in vampire films were relegated to either fainting in the corner and in need of male protection, or brainwashed slaves to a male master.

Female domination was also certainly a key factor involved in the performance of Celeste Yarnall as Diane Le Fanu, in Stephanie Rothman's *The Velvet Vampire*. Rothman, in an interview with Tony Williams, explained her motivation for the film and the choice to focus on a female vampire:

> We had a female vampire for two reasons. It was a commercial decision. We had just finished making *Student Nurses* which was a big success. The male buddy films were out. There was a correct hue and cry about the fact there were no more roles by women for women. Men came to see *Student Nurses* in droves. It was a mystery to me. Only later did I discover that the nurse is a very erotic figure in most male fantasies. There was a wide market out there for films about women and a very responsive audiences, not just men. *Student Nurses* was not a film designed exclusively for men. Many women came to see it. Therefore it was decided to make a horror film where all the main characters were women. I was in favor of this. Secondly, I'd seen horror films with women as victim and men as oppressor. It gets very tiresome and infuriating both to myself and many other women. So I decided that it was a great opportunity for equal time. (in Williams 1981: 87).

There has been much speculation over whether or not *The Velvet Vampire* was directly influenced by *Daughters of Darkness*. In her interview with Williams, Rothman indicated that the script — co-written with her husband Charles S. Swartz and originally titled *Through the Looking Glass* — took three to four months to complete. She also stated, 'We wanted to do something original', which would indicate she thought she was doing so at the time of writing (in Williams 1981: 86). If we consider the timing of when Kümel's film was released — May 1971 for the US — and add to that a period for producers at Roger Corman's New World Pictures to discuss making a similar film, Rothman's wish to create something unique, as well as the production timing, and then *The Velvet Vampire*'s eventual distribution and release — October 1971 — it seems highly unlikely this was the case. It appears to be a strange but genuine coincidence that the two films have fairly similar plots, in that they both contain a strong female vampire, who happens across a young couple and decides to interfere with their relationship because of an obsession the vampire has with the young girl in each consecutive pairing. For *The Velvet Vampire*, its main predator, Le Fanu, owns a desert ranch, and lures Lee (Michael Blodgett) and Susan Ritter (Sherry Miles) to stay with her, whereupon she embarks on psychological attacks towards Susan, invading her dreams at night — these set pieces take place on a billowing sand dune and feature the sublime use of a mirror and a bed — so she can take the girl as her own by breaking down her boundaries and spirit.

The film was puzzling to some audiences — especially for its apparent affiliation with arthouse cinema — and failed commercially. Rothman deliberately went against the grain found in general exploitation film of the period — the staple output of New World Pictures — and it is this factor that gives it a deeper alliance to *Daughters of Darkness*, far beyond likeness in their associated narratives. It can be argued that both films ultimately drink from the same well of tradition and inspiration; especially in their connection to the fantastic. While the director admits she was working predominantly with what she had, because, 'there were certain limitations in using live southern California locations where there were no vampire castles. We were going to be out in the bright desert sunlight', other aspects of the film were born from Rothman's own love of fantastic film. When asked about her influences, she stated, 'George Franju and Jean Cocteau. Since the French were influenced by American films it is only fair that an American should be influenced by the French. [...] Jean Cocteau once said, "When you look in the mirror you see your own death". That's the idea we worked with when the couple look in the mirror, behind which the vampire is observing them. Diane walks right out of the mirror on the sand and then to the bed' (in Williams 1981: 88).

In her article '*Daughters of Darkness*: Lesbian Vampires', Bonnie Zimmerman asserts:

> Although direct parallels between social forces and popular culture are risky at best, the popularity of the lesbian vampire film in the early 1970s may be related to the beginnings of an international feminist movement, as a result of which women began both to challenge male domination and to bond strongly with each other. Since feminism between 1970 and 1973 was not yet perceived as a fundamental threat, men could enjoy the sexual thrill provided by images of lesbian vampires stealing women and sometimes destroying men in the process. [...] The myth of the lesbian vampire, however, carries in it the potentiality for a feminist revision of meaning [...] The lesbian vampire film can lend itself to an even more extreme reading: that in turning to each other, women triumph over and destroy men themselves. One film that is considerably ambiguous about the lesbian vampire and thus lends itself particularly well to a feminist interpretation is DAUGHTERS OF DARKNESS. (1981: 24)

Zimmerman's observations, which will provide scope to analyse Kümel's film against another powerful lesbian vampire film from 1971, *The Blood Spattered Bride*, will be explored shortly. However, it is interesting that the writer selects *Daughters of Darkness* specifically to analyse in feminist terms, and not *The Velvet Vampire*, which by contrast to the male-directed feature was conceived with some awareness of feminist issues, through a female lens.

It is true that Kümel's film does welcome the aforementioned readings, because of the way it toys with gender and the themes of power and control, on what could be termed a feminist playing field. This said, Kümel has never declared himself intentionally feminist. It must be assumed that any spirit regarding this aspect found within the film, which when commented on almost always seems to relate to the performance by Delphine Seyrig, comes from the actress's own personal politics projected into the character, rather than any direct intention on the director's part. The year *Daughters of Darkness* was released, Seyrig was involved in a high-profile campaign for abortion rights in France. She also made feminist films both as an actress and director. Zimmerman's comments seem to support this notion, with the writer asserting, 'furthermore Delphine Seyrig is a very atypical lesbian vampire. She is a mature woman, unlike many other lesbian vampires who appear young and themselves vulnerable. This, in addition to her off-screen celebrity, gives her an aura of authority. She is never shown nude and is thus not vulnerable to male prurience as most lesbian vampires are' (ibid.). One has to wonder how different the film could have been if it hadn't been for Seyrig's performance, if it would have been made at all: the film is Delphine Seyrig, feminist politics and all, and for that genre cinema owes the actress a huge debt. This was a factor the actress appeared to be all too aware of.

Gothic Families: Outsiders, Monstrous Others, Subversion and Liberation

Even though the film deliberately subverts cinematic convention, when you strip the story down to its foundation, *Daughters of Darkness* is ultimately a classic Gothic tale. As such, it draws from a rich literary heritage through one of Gothic fiction's most dominant themes: a threat posed towards a family from an outsider or monstrous other.

Gothic literature began at a time when society was changing at a rapid pace. The period of the Enlightenment brought forth advances in science and industry. As a result, the social structure in Britain, and indeed the rest of Europe, was revolutionised, which in turn impacted on gender and class roles within the establishing patriarchal social hierarchy. With change came anxiety. Gothic offered a safe terrain to explore current fears of the time, especially for women. These anxieties were reflected in Gothic themes, such as the threat of contagion, violation and corruption, always from forces that penetrated the safe sanctuary of the family home. At the centre of the notion of 'home' was usually a heroine or maiden, who was at dire risk of having her morality corrupted or innocence shattered. Zimmerman argues,

> ...the lesbian vampire myth is a variation on the classic triangle: man and female vampire battling for possession of a woman. Pirie notes that lesbian vampire films such as *Daughters of Darkness* often incorporate the motif of the honeymoon [...] I would suggest that this is because the honeymoon, traditionally is a transitional period, during which the husband asserts his power and control over his bride, winning or forcing her into institutionalized heterosexuality. (2015: 78)

Daughters of Darkness takes this concept and uses it as a tool of subversion to break the rules, thus placing it in direct collusion with another transgressive film made the same year: Vicente Aranda's *The Blood Spattered Bride*. Both films explore the darker side of marriage — especially in terms of sexual violation and domestic violence — and place female vampires in the role of liberating figures for newlywed women who are faced with the prospect of living a life under the rule of a dominating, and aggressive, husband.

The Blood Spattered Bride differs from many of the films already discussed in this chapter for the way in which it is loaded with political and feminist subtext. Director Aranda, an important filmmaker in Spain, who started making films in the last decade of the Francoist regime (which ended with the dictator's death in 1975) and enjoyed a lengthy career in cinema — eventually upgrading from experimental satire and horror films to lush period dramas and literary epics — favoured strong female characters throughout his work, and used them to criticise the patriarchal system that dominated the social structure in his native homeland. Therefore, it is not surprising — that when you consider his body of cinema as a whole, and Aranda's status as an auteur — when he made a vampire film for his third solo feature length project, it was to Le Fanu's *Carmilla* he turned, and not Bram Stoker's *Dracula*.

Nonetheless, *The Blood Spattered Bride* strays wildly from Le Fanu's novella. Beginning with a young bride, Susan, clad in white, the initial scenes deliver a shocking graphic rape sequence, as the girl is violated by a masked intruder who enters her hotel room by force. While the audience learns shortly afterwards this is a nightmare, and hasn't actually occurred, it is a gruesome foreshadowing for what happens to the girl in her marital home, at the hands of her own husband (played by Simón Andreu). The husband isn't given a name in the credits. He can be read as representing patriarchy and male violence, in line with the Spanish political system of the era. Due to censorship constraints, filmmakers looking to criticise the fascist state had to adopt covert means in order to do so. Aranda used the metaphor of the female body, and violence inflicted on it by a husband protector figure, as his own way of addressing political problems within the regime. Susan therefore represents not just women — who were incredibly oppressed under Franco's state— but the whole Spanish nation crushed under fascism and patriarchy.

Moving politics to one side for a moment — a difficult task when analysing Aranda's film — *The Blood Spattered Bride*'s Susan and Valerie from *Daughters of Darkness* both represent the archetypal Gothic maiden. Innocent, wide-eyed and susceptible to corruption, the films subvert tradition by showing that the biggest threat to them doesn't really come from an invading other, as may be expected, but from within the sanctuary of their homes or marriages. 'The Husband' from *The Blood Spattered Bride*, shows his true colours on his wedding night, in a barbaric scene, which almost mirrors the fantasy violation shown at the start of the film. As the narrative develops he becomes increasingly more sadistic and cruel towards his new wife, whilst at the same time showing open concern for her declining mental health, eventually involving a doctor to diagnose her as suffering from neurosis, without acknowledging the impact domestic violence may be having on her mental state. Stefan from *Daughters of Darkness*, on the other hand, is slightly less open about his sadism — although the clues are there, especially in the way he relishes seeing the body of a woman found murdered in the local town, or his delight in recounting the crimes of Countess Bathory to his terrified wife. It is only when he feels threatened that he resorts to domestic violence, taking out his belt, and thrashing his wife into submission.

In *The Blood Spattered Bride* the vampiric Carmilla, an ancient descendent of 'The Husband' — himself human — first appears to Susan in dreams. As the film nears its second act, the girl is liberated in a dreamscape, whereby she is given a baptism with the blood of her husband, after she brutally stabs him to death with the help of the vampire. Carmilla then takes physical form, appearing in real life, and moving into the family home. Susan's lesbian relationship with the vampire is ultimately what sets her free. Thus, the constitution of marriage, and therefore patriarchal domination, is undermined by the coming together of two women in sexual union.

For *Daughters of Darkness*, Valerie, also trapped in a marriage with a husband she knows virtually nothing about, but soon learns he is prone to dark tempers, is also offered a way out by the arrival of a female vampire figure. Countess Bathory's motivation isn't as pure as Carmilla's would appear to be, however. It is certainly suggested by Ilona's behaviour, although not actually shown, that Valerie could be moving out of the frying pan and into the fire. This said, Valerie does not appear to have many other options. She is weak, and innocent, at the mercy of Stefan's outbursts or violent whims. Although she first rejects the Countess and her advances, after discovering Stefan is a cheat and has killed Ilona, the prospect of leaving with Bathory doesn't seem that awful after all. When the two women join forces, Stefan has lost, becoming powerless against them. He pays with his life for trying to assert otherwise.

Much of Stefan's anger spawns from the fact he has a secret. Stefan's mother, whom Valerie is desperate to meet, isn't quite what she seems. In fact, 'Lady Chiltern' is an older male, and possibly a lover, or Sugar Daddy, to Stefan. In a bizarre twist, Valerie's new husband may or may not be in the closet about his sexuality. Valerie assumes Stefan's reluctance to break the news to the person she believes is her new mother-in-law is down to the fact that he has married a person of lower class and his family are snobs, which couldn't be further from the truth. To move the discussion back to fairy tales again for one second, Stefan's secrecy, and his resulting behaviour, as Valerie gets closer to discovering what he is hiding, ties in nicely with Charles Perrault's Bluebeard, the moral of which is: wives should never poke their noses into their husband's business. To quote Perrault's text,

'Here,' said he, 'are the keys to the two great wardrobes, wherein I have my best furniture. These are to my silver and gold plate, which is not everyday in use. These open my strongboxes, which hold my money, both gold and silver; these my caskets of jewels. And this is the master key to all my apartments. But as for this little one here, it is the key to the closet at the end of the great hall on the ground floor. Open them all; go into each and every one of them, except that little closet, which I forbid you, and forbid it in such a manner that, if you happen to open it, you may expect my just anger and resentment.' (1697: no page)

Stefan's own 'anger and resentment' manifests through cruelty and the escalating domestic violence, which Valerie suffers at his hands. The closer she gets, the more spiteful he becomes. But it isn't a prince or father who comes to save her: it is Countess Bathory. Regardless of the fact that the countess has her own selfish reasons for getting involved with the girl, one has to ask, what is the alternative? Valerie's future with Stefan doesn't appear to be a bright one. If his explosive episodes in the first few days of marriage are any indication of where their relationship is going, Valerie looks set to go down a very dangerous road indeed.

In 1979, feminist author Angela Carter rewrote Perrault's stories for her book *The Bloody Chamber*, which included her own feminist take on Bluebeard. The writer empowered women and girls to become the heroes in their own journeys of self-discovery — often via a sexual awakening. Princes and fathers, who had previously arrived on the back of a white horse to rescue them, were replaced by strong female figures. In this sense, *Daughters of Darkness* can be read as being affiliated to *The Bloody Chamber*'s interpretation of the Bluebeard story, with Bathory standing in for the mother figure who crashes in to save the maiden at the end of Carter's subversive reworking. Much of this is again to do with actress Delphine Seyrig, as it was her decision to play the character 'all smiles', turning scripted violence into gentle caresses. Instead of an outright aggressor, she becomes something of a mother figure to Valerie. Many of Bathory's gestures are, although admittedly perversely, maternal towards the young girl. Ironically, Seyrig had already played a fairy godmother, and one with dubious intentions at that, in Jacque Demy's *Donkey Skin* (1970), the year before working on *Daughters of Darkness*. And while Demy's film, another adaptation of a Perrault tale, stays closer to tradition, both films flirt with subversion and transgression, albeit in different ways.

FOOTNOTES

2. For the most complete version to date, see the German DVD released in 2014..

Chapter Three: *Countess Dracula*

There is something especially profane about the Bathory myth, which seems to have deterred many filmmakers from attempting to approach the subject matter. Dracula (or Dracula's) is a far more romantic story, and in many ways a more conventional one, making it a lot easier to translate to the screen. Bathory, by contrast, is the tale of a blood-crazed woman who is said to have tortured 600-800 virgins to death, just for the hell of it. Tony Thorne makes a relevant point, in his own study, which attempts to document the historical facts concerning Bathory's story, *Countess Dracula*, in arguing,

> At least 320 films with a vampire theme were released between 1920 and 1990. Strangely, for a medium and a genre that have thrived on exaggeration, the handful of horror films which have been based on the legend of Elisabeth Bathory have shied away from confronting the enormity of her wickedness. A straightforward dramatisation of the crimes alleged against her in her lifetime — the murder of more than 600 women, genital mutilation, cannibalism — would entail a bloodbath — figuratively and literally — that would stretch the tolerance of the most liberal of end-of-century censors and risk unsettling even the most hardened aficionado of splatter movies. (2012: 18)

Logistical problems inherent in adapting the legend aside — bringing the numbers of potential victims down has been one way to tackle this issue on screen — outright aggressive, cruel and violent women have always been something of a taboo subject throughout Western culture. As Lucy Noakes argues, 'The binary distinction between the female life-giver and the male life-taker has been so widely naturalised that when women do kill, they are often seen as more ferocious and more dangerous than men' (2006: 10). To portray a female killer, who takes life because she enjoys it, who isn't punished, whose actions aren't explained away by curse, or neurosis, or feeble-mindedness, is to step right into realm of the taboo, which makes people uncomfortable. It is perhaps because of this that Bathory has not enjoyed as much celebration on screen as her male counterpart Dracula; himself in part said to be inspired by historical figure Vlad Tepes, aka Vlad the Impaler. However, as the very purpose of horror is often to explore the things that make us feel uncomfortable, to venture into the taboo in order to allow us to examine the darker side of humanity within a relatively safe space, figures like Bathory, who challenge the status quo by their very nature, are vital for the genre.

The aim of this chapter is to examine *Daughters of Darkness* in the context of its historical origins concerning the Bathory legend, as well as part of a small cinematic canon of like-minded films. The discussion will then open up to examine the themes of sadism, power, class and gender inherent in Kümel's film, some of which stem from the original legend, in order to establish just what makes *Daughters of Darkness* a truly transgressive piece of cinema.

THE REAL BLOOD COUNTESS

One person who wasn't afraid to dip their toe into the murky waters of the Bathory legend was French surrealist Valentine Penrose. The language employed in Penrose's part-fictional account of the life and times of Elizabeth Bathory, *Erzsebet Bathory, La Comtesse Sanglante* (1962), is deliberately evocative, highlighting the countess's wicked nature, as well as providing as an explicit link to the otherworldly and witchcraft, for sensational effect, which is an approach used throughout the text:

> Erzebet had been born there, in the East, within the mould of sorcery, in the shadow of the sacred crown of Hungary. In her there was nothing of the ordinary woman, who, instinctively, would flee in panic before demons. The demons were already in her: in the gloomy depths of her huge black eyes; and her face was pallid from their ancient poison. Her mouth was sinuous as a little snake, and her forehead was proud as the former was unflinching. (1962: 12)

It's the stuff of real horror stories. Penrose is equally as unflinching, in delivering all the grisly details of the woman's crimes, whilst asserting that the Countess acted under the influence of sorcery, which is one of the major themes of the book. While artistic flourish is often welcome in the retelling of gruesome legends, especially for those who love to gorge on the gory minutiae of human perversion, presentations such as these, where the line between fact and fiction becomes blurred, and myth and superstition melt into reality, make getting the real story of the infamous Blood Countess a difficult task indeed.

Tony Thorne, on the other hand, used only official documents, letters, and other paperwork, much of which was difficult to procure — with half of the story lost to the mists of time — in an attempt to construct a relatively accurate account of Bathory's life:

> The opportunity to explore the myth and reality of 'Countess Dracula' for the first time is an irresistible one for a writer. The persona of the Blood Countess is almost too rich in significance. She is two Jungian archetypes— the wicked stepmother and the fatal seductress — in one. She embodies so many modish end-of-century themes — she is an alleged murderess… a vampire, a woman wielding power in a man's world, and she is also from far away in time and place, so the Bathory biographer can fantasise that he is an early anthropologist, opening up new territory — in this case the forgotten Eastern half of the European continent and the communities of 400 years ago. (2012: 26)

As the previous quote highlights, the fact that Bathory lived over 400 years ago makes bringing the real truth to light somewhat problematic. There are the trial reports, and testimony of those accused of aiding the Countess, to consider when building up a picture of what actually happened. What becomes clear, through Thorne's patchwork of information, is that Bathory lived and reigned in a very different world to ours.

During her reigning years as Countess, Elizabeth Bathory was one of the most powerful women in Hungary. Her uncle was Stephen Bathory, King of Poland and Prince of Transylvania. In addition to this, her parents, Anna and George Bathory, were nobility of the highest order. Elizabeth's hand was pledged in marriage when she was just 10 years old to Ferenc Nádasdy, the marriage taking place when Elizabeth was 15. The coming together of two powerful Hungarian families was fortuitous for the young newly weds who are said to have acquired more wealth than the royal family through their legal union —— and in fact, according to Bathory historian Kimberly Craft (2009), the couple would often lend money to the Royal Court, much of which was not given back. Ferenc would go on to become a decorated war hero, notoriously cruel and ruthless in his methods. He spent most of his married life seperated from his wife, as he fought in battle against invading Turk armies, which earned him the nickname the Black Knight of Hungary.

It was after Ferenc's death that Bathory's crimes are reported to have become more prominent, although, as Craft explains, the countess already had a record for being needlessly cruel to her servants before she became a widow. However, as historians such as Thorne have explored — and it's also a subject that becomes the main plot line for Juraj Jakubisko's multi-million dollar period epic *Bathory* (2008) — Elizabeth Bathory was a powerful woman in a time when women had very little legal or financial power. Because her husband was away at war for large portions of their time together, it was up to Elizabeth to run their sprawling estates, which at one time was composed of over 16 castles alone. Therefore, she was a woman who could hold her own in a man's world. Even after her husband's death, when it was customary for wealth to transfer to male relatives, Elizabeth held on to her position, and demonstrated time after time that she would not bow down to any man. She built up a close team of cohorts and aides, mainly women, many of whom were implicated in her crimes. And because of this, as Thorne and Jakubisko have both suggested (although the film by the latter is hardly historically accurate, given it proposes the countess had an affair with Italian painter Caravaggio), the accusations against Bathory could very well have been an attempt to strip the woman of her wealth and power. György Thurzó, Palatine of Hungary, the man tasked with investigating local reports of the Countess' crimes — previously a family friend to the Nádasdys — certainly had a vested interest in the case, given that he was able to further his own political and financial position through the arrest of Elizabeth and her collaborators.

Whether events were invented, exaggerated, or not — and the idea of the countess bathing in the blood of her victims almost certainly seems to be a fabrication when you consider it does not appear in any of the numerous testimonies given to the court during her trial — what remains is the fact that the arrest of Elizabeth Bathory was a highly political move. And while the details of Bathory's crimes have since moved into the realm of legend, to be written and rewritten over centuries, her position as a aristocratic noblewomen who possessed great power cannot be denied. Kümel's film, as we shall see in this chapter, explores the concept of class and power perhaps more than any other Bathory-based film of its era. He also uses the idea of the Hungarian 16th aristocracy as inherently sadistic, a context which is historically correct if records are to be believed, to produce one of the most ruthless female monsters to come out of the canon of seventies vampire films, even if he fleshes out other aspects of the story with supernatural and fantastical notes.

BATHORY IN FILM

A COUNTESS IN NAME ONLY

Prior to Elizabeth Bathory becoming an intellectual asset ripe for adaptation to horror film, her presence in cinema seems to have been somewhat more abstract. For instance, there is an obscure Czechoslovakian feature titled *Odhalenie Alzbety Báthorycky* (1965), which purports to be something of satirical comedy, playing along the lines of a film within in a film. The film was apparently taken off its theatrical run after no more than twenty showings. Like so much of Czechoslovakian cinema from this period the narrative appears to act as a foundation to critique a culture oppressed under communism through absurdist comedy. The film has little in common with either the real story of Countess Bathory or any of the fictional horror films that followed in her name.

Likewise, Franco Bracani's utterly strange 'statement' film *Necropolis* (1970) has virtually no resemblance to the historical Bathory either. The loose connection comes through a character played by Warhol Superstar Viva Hoffman, who, while not explicitly named 'Countess Bathory', appears to be inspired (at least in a small way) by her. Bracani's film is a surreal, fragmented, free-form series of monologues, with no discernable narrative or plot. Mainly it flows from one set piece to another, where characters offer up statements, many of which have even less meaning than the narrative itself. At one point, actor Pierre Clémenti, after giving a rousing speech, straddles a horse, with his naked body on display leaving little to the imagination. Carmelo Bene (who had previously appeared in Pier Paolo Pasolini's *Oedipus Rex*, 1967) makes an appearance supposedly as The Devil. There is another part for 'Frankenstein's Monster', which is played by Bruno Corazzari.

Viva's 'Bathory' is initially introduced giving a long rambling improvised monologue, in which she cuckolds a male character in the room with her, commenting on his impotence and her need for sex, which he can't or won't provide. This then moves into another scene where the actress is seen reading from an unnamed book — the prose of which is evocative of Penrose — recounting the crimes of Countess Bathory. Viva is also seen tying up one woman's wrists, and seductively groping another.

What remains interesting about these two films, which have little in common with Kümel's feature, is the fact that they are both highly politicised, using Bathory as something of a metaphorical statement, much like the real countess if you interpret her story as one relating to political power and conspiracy. It is also important to note these films preceded any horror adaptations of the myth. When *Daughters of Darkness* was made, the story was still a relatively new concept for horror, despite the fact many other female focused vampire films were being made around the same time.

BATHORY AS A HORROR ICON

Hammer Films' *Countess Dracula* (1971) was one of the first films to take the subject matter fully into straight up horrific territory, giving events a supernatural twist just for good measure. Working from ideas found in the work of Valentine Penrose, Countess Bathory (Ingrid Pitt) — renamed in the film title '*Countess Dracula*' to cash in on the studio's long-running and highly popular franchise — uses witchcraft and the blood of young virgins to revitalise her aging skin. Bathory convinces a young suitor she is a maiden, by posing as her own daughter, and is intent on marrying him, her lust and vanity motivating her to take the lives of an increasing number of innocent women. The countess then finds herself locked in a perpetual cycle of aging and regeneration, with every new kill. She will stop at nothing to look younger and get the man she desires, even if it means putting her own daughter at risk of harm.

Ingrid Pitt took up the role of the infamous Blood Countess, capitalising on the success she had with Hammer previously, when she played Carmilla Karnstein for their Carmilla adaptation, *The Vampire Lovers*. However, the Bathory of *Countess Dracula* is markedly different from the sexual predator seen in *The Vampire Lovers*, even if Pitt portrays the character with more than a hint of sadism. Instead, the focus is on giddy enthusiasm, and utter delusion, as a woman is driven to take the lives of a number of girls because she gets so caught up in her own narcissistic fantasy, in which she frantically struggles to turn back the clock on old age in order to regain her lost youth. Despite this, and the fact she is a woman of power, Pitt's character is seen to rely on the men around her, and is a far cry from the ruthless aristocratic noble woman seen in historical accounts. If we compare Pitt's Bathory to Seyrig's, we find they are completely different animals indeed. Pitt does have her moments of cold-hearted calculation, but is driven at a maddening pace by the fact that just a few hours after she has bathed in blood, she begins to age once again. Seyrig's Countess doesn't suffer this problem — while she too is compelled to drink blood, it doesn't seem to be a matter of urgency for her. Instead the narrative allows her the space to develop her sadistic games at a somewhat leisurely pace.

Jorg Grau's *Blood Ceremony* (1973) is another film which takes its lead from the Hammer formula, rather than from Kümel's. As a Spanish horror film from the Eurocult school of seventies filmmaking, the focus is on sexuality and blood, as opposed to drama and historical accuracy. Grau's film, in a similar fashion to the aforementioned Hammer feature, focuses heavily on the magic and mysticism line found in the pages of Penrose's text, making much more of the witchcraft angle than Peter Sasdy (the director of *Countess Dracula*) was able to. The result is an enjoyable, earthy, sexualised romp into the world of Bathory, combined with a body-count-by-numbers formula. The killings are amongst the most graphic in the Bathory canon, with victims bled from the throat, like animal carcasses. Their blood is then fed through a hole in the ceiling so that the Countess might bathe in it. Just like *Countess Dracula*, *Blood Ceremony*'s Bathory is another fragile creature, one who is largely at the mercy of her own whims and fantasies, making her, again, unlike the portrayal by Delphine Seyrig in *Daughters of Darkness*, who by contrast is someone fully in control of her own destiny and power games.

In addition to Grau's feature, two of Paul Naschy's werewolf films draw inspiration from the legend. In León Klimovsky's *La Noche de Walpurgis* (*The Werewolf vs. The Vampire Woman*, 1971) Naschy's doomed lycanthrope Waldemar Daninsky has to fight against a medieval serial killer, and vampire, Countess Wandesa Dárvula de Nadasdy (Patty Shepard), who has been unearthed from her grave by two nubile young students (Gaby Fuchs as Elvira, and Barbara Capell as Genevieve Bennett). Although Klimovsky's undead countess isn't given the Bathory name specifically, the character's name 'Nadasdy' bears a reference to the family of Elizabeth's husband, Ferenc — Jess Franco also adopted this name for Soledad Miranda's character in *Vampyros Lesbos*, which was explored in the previous chapter. Naschy would loosely remake the film himself, in 1980, under the title of *El Retorno del Hombre Lobo* (*The Return of the Wolfman*), changing the name Nadasdy to Elisabeth Bathory (played by Julia Saly), and adding that all-important Penrosian witchcraft angle. While these two films play on the Blood Countess legend as a form of overtly Gothic supernatural horror, they do share a certain affinity to *Daughters of Darkness*, in that, for Naschy's films the Bathory figure is purely a force of power in her own right — not motivated by vanity, or influenced by other people — as is Seyrig's Bathory in Kümel's film. Similarly, this power is used as a force to hypnotise, take control of, and otherwise turn young women into brainwashed slaves and vampires themselves.

THE ART OF COUNTESS BATHORY

Part of the irony in Kümel's motive to make a film that aligned with popular exploitation cinema of the period is that *Daughters of Darkness* stands out from that herd because it connects far more with European arthouse film than it does exploitation. Critics usually pick out the more artistic elements of the film to lavish praise on, such as the director's keen eye for colour motifs and the use of other subliminal touches like the hidden subtext found in his use of flowers to denote certain themes. Delphine Seyrig's own reputation only strengthens this association; she is an actress linked with the work of critically acclaimed auteurs.

On this basis, it could be argued that *Daughters of Darkness* has far more in common with the work of, for example, Walerian Borowczyk and Miklós Jancsó than it does with Peter Sasdy's *Countess Dracula* or any of the Spanish horror films which were inspired by the Bathory name. Like Kümel, Polish-born Borowczyk and Hungarian Jancsó were directors who had previously impressed critics with 'serious art films' before moving to incorporate softcore sex into some of their pictures (Jancsó used orgies and copious amounts of nudity to make a political statement in *Private Vices, Public Virtues* [1976]; whilst Borowczyk, from *Immoral Tales* [1973] and *The Beast* [1975] onwards, reveled in sex, and occasionally violence too). Despite the shift in focus, each director, Kümel, Borowczyk and Jancsó, managed to keep their auterist signatures intact, turning erotic film into an artistic statement and proving there really is no such thing as a concrete high/low divide when it comes to cinema. Both Kümel and Borowczyk would later go on to direct episodes of an erotic French television series, *Série rose* (which aired in the US as *Softly from Paris*, 1986-1991), with Kümel adapting stories from Nicolas Restif de La Bretonne, Marguerite de Navarre, Niccolò Machiavelli and Guy de Maupassant, and Borowczyk, Nicolas Restif de La Bretonne and Giovanni Boccaccio. The series is a good example of how the two directors stand more or less on the same page when it comes to mixing decadent themes, art and eroticism; although admittedly, Kümel's film work has never been as graphic as Borowczyk's when it comes to sexual content.

Borowczyk's own adaptation of the Bathory story is quite unlike many of the horror films being made around the same time. The 30-minute short is one of the chapters that made up *Immoral Tales*, starring Paloma Picasso as the infamous Blood Countess. The story plays out more along the lines of a drama with elements of horror and eroticism. Bathory's young aide, a girl disguised as a male named Istvan (Pascale Christophe), is sent to the local village to collect girls for the countess. The locals try and hide their daughters, but to no avail. The girls are found and lined up, with the youngest and prettiest selected to attend the Bathory residence. Once there, they are made to shower. Thinking it's all part of a game, the unwitting girls appear to be in good spirits. As they are led to the countess' bed chamber excitement turns to hysteria, and things take a horrific turn for the worst in the expected fashion. Borowczyk avoids the typical horror tropes of neck biting, or even cruelty and torture methods, instead choosing to make his point by cutting away to the countess bathing in blood. In order to achieve authenticity, the director reportedly used pig's blood for the scene, thus making it stand out against the faker looking (more genre oriented) Bathory histories on screen, where bright red stage blood is usually employed.

At first glance it might be easy to draw a connection between *Daughters of Darkness* and the Bathory of *Immoral Tales* through the most obvious route concerning their respective approaches to eroticism, with both films placing more emphasis on an artful direction than many of the horror exploitation pictures of the period. And while this may be correct, at least to a certain extent, Borowczyk and Kümel's narratives unite on a much deeper level; the key to which can be found within the interpersonal relationships between of some of their key players. Both directors chose to portray Bathory as true to her history, as a callous aristocrat and somewhat emotionally detached from her actions, viewing lower-order people as servants, or in the case of Kümel's film, a minor annoyance, who should know their place. Yet, conversely, the women also demonstrate an intense desire to be worshipped, and they do this by enslaving their assistants, so that they may not only fulfill their blood lust, but their emotional and sexual needs too.

Although Bathory's assistant in *Immoral Tales* appears to have power in her position — the power to select young girls from the village; the privilege of sharing a bed with her master (as Ilona does in *Daughters of Darkness*) — it is still very clear who is in charge of the relationship, and when stripped down to its core, the dynamic can be seen as nothing more than one of master and slave. Any suggestion of romance is in fact built on a bed of coercion and resentment. We see this exact same feeling of bitterness found in the behaviour of Bathory's companion in *Immoral Tales* — as well as an obvious desire to be free from enslavement — in Ilona's character in *Daughters of Darkness*. Bathory responds in a way that reinforces the reality of the situation, demonstrating quite clearly the girl has no choice or agency in her current situation. Ilona, like Istvan in *Immoral Tales* is there by contract, subservient to the countess.

In the case of *Daughters of Darkness*, this dynamic is repeated again in Bathory's relationship with Valerie, another lower-class person with whom the Countess develops a strange infatuation. Brigid Cherry describes this as stemming from 'Elizabeth's superior aristocratic attitudes toward others', continuing,

> She [Bathory] is controlling, as when Ilona tries to leave her and Valerie tries to reject her advances. Her demand that 'You must be nice to me; soon you'll love me as I love you now' after kissing Valerie's palm and leaving the imprint of her red lips can be read as of the dominant aristocratic demands on inferiors, staff and servants, and even lovers. Even though Valerie says she despises her (as her serfs might despise their master) Elizabeth will not let her go — she claims ownership of Valerie. (2014: 228)

If you take these two films and then compare them to everything else in the Bathory filmic universe, especially those features that sit unambiguously in the horror and exploitation fields, one thing that becomes startlingly obvious is that none of the others appear to possess this particular dynamic: a close bond between Bathory and her female confidante that could otherwise be described as a Sadean relationship angle, one based on the power structures involved in social class. For example, in Hammer's

Countess Dracula the Bathory figure is cruel to her servants, but she does not develop any kind of emotional bond with them at all, keeping a distinct distance (although they are still slaves, there is a lack of a Sadeian angle). Instead, her ardour is turned towards other members of the nobility. And in other films, such as the Spanish horrors previously mentioned in this chapter, Bathory either works alone, and then brainwashes her minions — in the way Count Dracula would — or in the case of *Blood Ceremony*, she is seen working with a witch but does not take up any sort of sexual or romantic relationship with the woman.

Final mention in the arthouse bracket does need to go to Jancsó's highly surreal *The Tyrant's Heart, or Boccaccio in Hungary* (1981), which appears modelled more on films like *Fellini Satyricon* (1969) than anything in the Bathory canon. Teresa Ann Savoy — who had previously starred in the director's *Private Vices, Public Virtues* — is cast as Bathory; this time modelled as an incestuous vampire of sorts, and mother to the central protagonist. The film couldn't be any more different to *Daughters of Darkness* in style and substance, but its emphasis on eroticism and striking visuals does put them in the same camp to some degree. Both films also play with the notion of decadence and the aristocracy. However, unlike Kümel's vision, Jancsó's film holds little appeal to genre fans.

DE SADE, CRUELTY, POWER AND CLASS

As far as the Bathory legend goes, especially as an increasing amount of time goes by, the episodes which led to the arrest of the countess have been wildly exaggerated and taken out of context. For example, the Guinness Book of Records holds the countess on record as being 'The most prolific female murderer and the most prolific murderer of the western world' (n.d.), stating that Bathory 'practised vampirism on girls and young women. She is alleged to have killed more than 600 virgins in order to drink their blood and bathe in it, ostensibly to preserve her youth' (n.d.). Yet, no evidence of vampirism has ever been found in any of the official reports of her crimes, and the number, while still high, has been placed as much lower — if court testimony is to be believed, anywhere between 60-200 — by serious scholars who have studied the facts surrounding the Bathory case in some depth.

Getting a clear picture is easier said than done. Modern historians attempting to solve the mystery of what actually happened have found the research processes complicated and fraught with difficulties. For the two major historical studies which exist at the time of writing this book, those by Tony Thorne and Kimberley Craft, the respective writers accessed archives in Hungary, churning over hundreds of letters, court reports and testimony, much like a modern day detective would, in order to fit together the clues. A lot of the material has been found to be incomplete, leaving nothing but the imagination or speculation to fill in the gaps. To add in extra complications, all testimony has to be viewed with a critical eye, given the fact that, as was par for the course during the era, it is likely that the first-hand evidence — for example, the confessions from Bathory's circle of helpers — was gathered under extreme conditions: torture, deprivation and fear. That's not to say there is no story there. Indeed, despite these issues some consistencies can be found.

The picture which emerges shows that Bathory's motive for her crimes was likely to have been far more mundane that the whisperings of witchcraft and blood-filled baths which surround the legend today; less sensational, perhaps, but in a way far more horrific. It's easier to understand a serial killer under the terms of pathology: in Bathory's case a woman so mad as to believe she can stay young forever by killing young virgins, and then bathing in vats of their blood. The 'real' case of Countess Bathory tells an entirely different story altogether.

Unless it is understood that a culture of cruelty — not violence, but deliberate cruelty — was endemic in the era that has come to be known as the early modern, the Bathory story cannot be unravelled. The celebration of this culture has something common to all of Europe at the time and its practice had been embedded in Hungarian life, almost institutionalised, since the atrocities suffered by the peasantry in the early sixteenth century. Treacherous, rapacious nobles brutalised their own countrymen for short-term advantage and ignored the long-term effects on the prosperity and vitality of the whole nation. (Craft 2009: 449)

What this culture of cruelty translates to in the case of Countess Bathory is systematic, sustained, violence toward her staff — many of whom were young girls brought into her home to serve her — in the name of enforcing order and compliance. Allegations in the original documents, despite discrepancies over numbers, do build a coherent view, with witness testimony corroborating the confessions of Bathory's collaborators. The catalogue of crimes listed include (but are not limited to): excessive beatings or torture as punishment for minor infractions — for instance, a girl who was found to have stolen money had a coin burned into her hand — and very much more of the same for anything that was seen as resistance to following orders; including slowness caused by tiredness or less than perfect work. A number of the reports cited by Craft and Thorne suggest girls were regularly stripped naked and exposed to the elements; for example, made to stand outside in cold water up to the necks for hours at a time, or left out in brutal winter weather conditions without clothing. Tools were employed to carry out torture such as pincers and pokers. It was commonplace for Bathory's team of collaborators to implement the violent acts supposedly at their master's request. Girls were regularly seen at the castle beaten black and blue, or in various states of bad health due to impoverished living conditions, which only added to the ill-effects of constant abuse. Food and sleep were often withheld from the girls as a form of torture. Other violent acts, such as biting (not in a vampiric way) and pinching, were reported across several witness statements. The countess would often resort to verbal humiliation whilst carrying out punishments, mocking the girls or insulting them with terms like 'whore'.

Even though people were appalled with Bathory's behaviour at the time of her arrest, when you consider the context of her crimes, it becomes understandable. Bathory lived in an era where a feudal system operated, meaning lower class people were considered serfs or peasants, property of their respective lords and ladies, who dehumanised them as a result. It is also widely considered that the countess learned some of her behaviour from her husband, who set a ruthless example:

> ... stories already circulated amongst the servants that he [Ferenc Nadasdy], too, enjoyed torturing servants and teaching his wife ways in which to discipline them. He was already known to be ruthless on the battlefield and sought retribution against his enemies in atrocious ways. At least once, he ordered the execution of captured prisoners 'in the most heinous way possible.' He was also known to dance with the dead bodies of his enemies and throw their severed heads into the air to play 'catch' and kickball with them. (Craft 2009)

The overwhelming sentiment we can take from this information amounts to an obvious feeling of entitlement inherent in the mindset of nobility of the period. This exact same attitude lies at the very core of Kümel's film. *Daughters of Darkness* may also riff on popular vampire myth seen in cinema of the era, as well as the notion that the countess, as an immortal, needs blood to stay young, but the very thing that makes Seyrig's character so compelling comes from a historical basis: she is a narcissist who views herself above all others by birthright, not a damned creature, or agent of Satan, or even a vampire tortured by a curse. This not only ties her to an interesting historical perspective, but it also makes her a particularly unique figure in cinema too, especially when her gender is taken into account.

Ironically, as suggested by Craft, the real life Bathory's crimes finally caught up with her because she became too careless about events which were happening under her command and started to attack girls of a higher social class. She felt she was so powerful that she was above the law. Bathory in *Daughters of Darkness* appears to hold this same disdain for any authority figure who dares to question her or interfere with her business; this is evident in the way she treats both the retired cop and the concierge.

What becomes really interesting about the class aspect in Kumel's film is its direct link to literature, with the director apparently rejecting the atypical 'female' vampire found in *Carmilla*, in favour of a more masculine decadent model. As Brigid Cherry observes:

> The roots and history of vampire fiction also cast the gothic vampire in the hierarchy of the social order, notably as a decadent aristocrat, Countess Bathory being the female counterpart to Count Dracula (both vampire narratives drawing on bloodthirsty historical rulers from Eastern Europe). Elizabeth's costumes in Daughters of Darkness directly connect her with moneyed and leisured aristocracy. In her position as a titled woman of leisure drifting around Europe, Elizabeth is akin to Byron's Augustus Darvell and Polidori's Lord Ruthven — 'vampire dandies created by nineteenth century bohemians' as Milly Williamson describes them. (Cherry 2014: 227)

In many ways the film can be seen as a natural forerunner to Anne Rice's *Interview with the Vampire*, which would be published four years later in 1976. Although Rice's novel embraces certain aspects of Gothic ruin — the very things *Daughters of Darkness* rejects — the main protagonist, Lestat, holds many of the same characteristics as Seyrig's Bathory. Lestat is fuelled not only by blood lust, but a penchant for fine living. He seems to live by Bathory's motto: 'nothing in life is ever serious'. Companionship in both *Daughters of Darkness* and *Interview with the Vampire* takes on a deeply existential level, and there is a relationship with cruelty found in both vampires that appears to transcend the conventions that dictate vampires are violent because of an animalistic predatory drive. These vampires torture because they enjoy it. In fact, in the case of *Daughters of Darkness*, this primal level of vampirism is completely excluded from the narrative. Bathory is cruel because she wants to be, and most importantly because she can afford to be, not because she needs to be.

In favouring cruelty over primality *Daughters of Darkness* opens itself up to other possibilities: those with a distinctly Sadeian flavour. Bathory isn't just a wealthy socialite, a direct descendant to the Gothic dandies and Byronic heroes, as suggested by Cherry, she's an outright libertine too — this is another aspect she shares in common with Rice's Lestat.

It is through reading the elements of de Sade inherent in *Daughters of Darkness*, especially when informed by the writing of Angela Carter, that its most feminist inclinations become apparent. In *Sadeian Women and Ideology of Pornography* (1978), Carter argues,

> He [Sade] enlarges the relation between activity and passivity in the sexual act to include tyranny and the acceptance of physical and political oppression. The great men in his novels, the statesmen, the princes, the popes, are the cruelest by far and their sexual voracity is a kind of pure destructiveness; they would fuck the world and fucking, for them, is the enforcement of annihilation... But his great women, Juliette, Clairwill, the Princess Borghese, Catherine the Great of Russia, Charlotte of Naples, are even more cruel still since, once they have tasted power they know how to use their sexuality as an instrument of aggression... A free woman in an unfree society will be a monster. Her freedom will be a condition of personal privilege that deprives those on which she exercises it of her own freedom. The most extreme kind of this deprivation is murder. These women murder. (1978: 27)

Kümel's Bathory certainly fits this mould. She is a monster in every sense of the word, even if the director only insinuates the great darkness that lurks within her. Kümel takes a similar approach to sex, leaving much for the viewer to read between the lines, but it is clear that Bathory's power is also tied to this aspect of her persona, and power play is linked not so much to money — although this clearly provides Bathory with the freedom to travel and gives her a sense of entitlement — but seduction and sexuality. In this respect, Countess Bathory is the ultimate Sadeian Woman, being someone who has expertly learned to navigate the world using sex as an instrument for destruction. Unlike Countess Dracula, or even Carmilla, she is not at the mercy of an uncontrollable libidinal energy. Instead, she understands that this energy can be used as a tool of oppression, aggression and manipulation, and has spent centuries refining her technique, thus making her unstoppable when it comes to getting what she wants.

Daughters of Darkness arguably anticipates Rainer Werner Fassbinder's *The Bitter Tears of Petra Von Kant* (1972), which was based on Fassbinder's own play. Fassbinder's film, while not horror, exhibits the same sense of claustrophobia evident in Kümel's film, which stems largely from the themes of obsession, sadism and co-dependency inherent in the narrative, as much as it does the power games played out on a landscape dominated by female characters. It is perhaps not surprising, given the similarities between Petra Von Kant and Countess Bathory that the actress Delphine Seyrig would go on to play Petra on the stage in a production for New End Theatre Hampstead in 1977, where she was paired with Angela Pleasence (from *Symptoms*, 1974), and Jenny Runnacre (the star of Dereck Jarman's *Jubilee*, 1978). Fassbinder's 1972 filmic adaptation of the play stars Margit Carstensten as the titular Petra, a recently divorced fashion designer. Exclusively seen in her bedroom, which also doubles up as a lounge and office, Petra is often seen barking out orders to her assistant Marlene (Irm Hermann); the latter, who seems to suffer in passive silence, caters to her employer's every whim, even completing her design work for her. Petra's demands frequently border on sadism, with Marlene taking the role of the servile masochist — not unlike the dynamic between Ilona and Bathory (although Petra is a lot harsher in her attention toward her own secretary). While the character of Petra is much more fragile than Countess Bathory, they do share some of the same character traits when it comes to the type of skills they employ in the manipulation of their charges. Similarly, they are both narcissists, demanding to be loved by the women they try to control, which in both cases reaches sickly suffocating heights of obsession. Likewise, Petra, like Bathory, is an older woman, who uses her power, wisdom, and money, to her advantage, and is often seen flipping between maternal protector, insecure demanding lover, and cruel manipulator in order to get what she wants.

BLOOD HARVEST: THE CULT OF COUNTESS BATHORY

The subject of social class is a particularly relevant one when taken in the political context of the era in which *Daughters of Darkness* was made. Toward the end of the 1960s, and into the early '70s, civil unrest, especially amongst students and young people, was exploding all over the western world. This resulted in a variety of protests, which were often violent, especially in Europe and America, as people expressed the frustration they felt at war, capitalism and civil rights violations. As a result, there were a number of genre films made around the turn of the decade that took a satirical approach to presenting their subject matter and reflected or criticised social issues of the time. In Italy in particular, where wealthy industrialists were increasingly being accused of corruption and exploitation of workers, there emerged a prevalence of rotten aristocratic decadent villains in horror films — most notably in the *giallo* cycle — the likes of which can be understood in terms of exposing the evils of capitalism, privilege and wealth.

Within this very specific social context the vampire becomes the perfect metaphor for powerful and wealthy people or establishments, who literally suck the lifeblood out of those they exploit in order to retain their positions of privilege. Films of note which cover this theme made within the period include Corrado Farina's cynical 1971 feature *Hanno cambiato faccia* (*They Have Changed Their Face*), which concerns itself with using the vampire as a symbol for capitalism. For Farina, the vampire is not so much the Gothic bloodsucker of old, but instead, a high-powered executive coming up with advertising campaigns in order to brainwash the masses. Within the narrative vampires attack counterculture and anti-establishment values, and villainy is associated with the coerced assimilation with capitalist ideals. Tonino Cervi's *Queens of Evil* (1970) took a similar route, but used witches, instead of vampires, to reflect more or less the same point of view.

Meanwhile, Jean Rollin's *La Vampire Nue* (1970) partly focuses on a suicide cult, which operates from a bourgeois Parisian townhouse. The collective is run by a corrupt businessman, who is found to be keeping a vampire prisoner so that he may learn her secret of eternal life. In order to feed her he tricks cult members into giving up their own lives, in order to provide a ready supply of fresh blood. The members believe they are doing so for a higher purpose, but the truth is it's all about one man's greed and selfish desire.

Although it does not feature vampires of the supernatural kind, offbeat *giallo* film *The Bloodstained Lawn* (1973) (which also incorporates elements of science fiction) casts an equally critical eye on the subject of power and privilege. Marina Malfatti and Enzo Tarascio star as an eccentric, rich and ruthless couple, who lure unsuspecting victims to their secluded mansion so that they may drain their bodies for blood. Generally the people they ensnare are considered socially unacceptable by the couple; people who stand in direct opposition to their bourgeoisie values — for instance, a pair of hippies and a tramp are among those who are targeted as appropriate fodder for the bizarre industry.

Alain Jessua's *Shock Treatment* (1973) is another film which mines this particular vein. Set at a state of the art health spa, run by the enigmatic Docteur Devilers (Alain Delon), members of the social elite who lodge there are offered his mysterious miracle treatment, which reverses the effects of aging without the need for plastic surgery. Jessua's film also offers up some thought-provoking commentary on cheap migrant labour for extra measure.

1979's *Thirst*, directed by Rod Hardy, has much in common with Jessua's film, but goes further, bringing in Bathory specifically — or at least her name — by introducing members of her bloodline, who are operating a global organisation called The Brotherhood. The Brotherhood maintain their supply of sustenance by farming people who are kept there by coercion and manipulation, in a large high-tech facility that resembles a spa or sanitarium and houses 'milking' machinery for blood-letting. The idea of Bathory as a godlike figurehead for a cult had already been used in Joe Sarno's *Vampire Ecstasy* (1973), but that particular film came with no overt political messages. *Thirst*, on the other hand, is teeming with them. As one high-ranking member explains, 'We are a simply a superior race of people who over the centuries have proved that the drinking of the vital human essence confers youth, power. It's the ultimate aristocratic act.' Once again we are back to the core of Bathory's historical story, and the idea of heritage and entitlement. One could almost imagination Seyrig's Countess speaking this line herself.

Daughters of Darkness may not deliberately channel the social climate of the era, but it does own a very small place in this subset of films because of the obvious class aspects inherent in the narrative. Kümel may not have been as cynical as many of the filmmakers mentioned here, but he was certainly on the same page when it came to exposing the rotten core of wealth and privilege.

Chapter Four: Twins of Evil

Just as with cinema, classic vampire literature has been traditionally dominated by an intense focus on male-centric narratives. The ultimate book, the one from which many artists have taken their inspiration, including filmmakers, is Bram Stoker's *Dracula*. Count Dracula has ruled supreme as the Grandmaster vampire pretty much since the book's publication in 1897. As mentioned in Chapter Two, the earliest horror films then looked to Stoker's text to build their model of vampirism on screen. Female vampires, as in the case of *Dracula's Daughter* for example, were cast as assistants, minions or lower order beings, who were subservient to a higher male power. In the case of the aforementioned Universal sequel to the original forerunner, the vampire is the offspring of the infamous count, and a woman who fails to embrace her supernatural power as an immortal, instead viewing her current state of being as a curse from which she needs to escape, lest she live out an endless life tormented by what she considers an affliction.

When we look back into the annals of Gothic literature and delve past the overwhelming shadow of Stoker's creation, another picture becomes clear: vampires didn't begin as exclusively male, at least not in a literary sense, and especially not in a mythical one. As we have seen in the previous chapter, *Daughters of Darkness* is unique in that it uses the essence of contemporary male vampires — the monied dandy model — to instill very masculine qualities in Bathory's character, despite the fact she is gendered female. This approach is in keeping with the historical accounts of the countess that illustrate she was a capable, hardened woman, who was forced to survive in a harsh and violent man's world. However, as this chapter will reveal, these aren't the only links in Kümel's film to a literary sphere. Even though the director states he wasn't looking to books like Le Fanu's *Carmilla* to inform him when he wrote the screenplay for the film, he does admit to having read it. Taking this into consideration it isn't surprising that some parallels can be made between the film and Le Fanu's text.

As this chapter will show, *Daughters of Darkness* not only shares an affiliation to the likes of *Carmilla*, ancient myth, and some of the earliest examples of female vampires in literature, such as Coleridge's Christabel, but it also delves into the territory of fin de siècle decadent writers, in particular Charles Baudelaire, Jean Lorrain and Jules Barbey d'Aurevilly.

MYTH, MONSTROSITY AND MOTHERHOOD

By tracking the evolution of the vampire from its ancient to modern incarnations, historian Sir Christopher Frayling explains,

> The vampire is as old as the world… Blood drained by the Lamiae, emissaries of the Triple Goddess Hecate; blood sucked by Lilith, the other woman in Adam's life; blood shed for the dead Attis and mourning Cybele, the Great Mother; blood as taboo… But the family tree of card-carrying vampire of modern European fictions — the great saigneur, combining the beauty of Milton's Satan with the haughtiness of Byron's Fatal Man — as opposed to the genesis of the myth itself, is relatively accessible. Some of the early Romantics, such as Burger, Goethe and Keats, based their vampire visions (loosely) on classical Greek and Roman manifestations. More often, vampire tales and poems in the nineteenth century were derived from folktales and eye witness accounts of 'posthumous magic. (Frayling 1992: 5)

Through centuries of writing, and rewriting, the legend of Bathory has become so exaggerated it is now nothing more than a folk tale itself. Kümel retains many of these mythical aspects for his film, in order to present the story as fantasy and escapism, rather than cold hard fact. In line with this approach, *Daughters of Darkness* owes a partial debt to a much older myth than seventeenth-century serial killer yarns. And, it is this aspect that makes *Daughters of Darkness* so fascinating, in comparison to the bulk of similar female vampire films from the same period.

Within Jewish mythology, Lilith — Adam's first wife, who was apparently cast out of the Garden of Eden because she refused to bow down to her male counterpart — presents two faces, both of them equally dangerous. Scholar Sigmund Hurwitz describes this in terms of a 'dual aspect', stating, 'depending on whether she is faced with a man or a woman, one or other side of her becomes more apparent. When she is a faced with a man, the aspect of the *divine whore*, or, psychologically speaking, that of the seductive anima comes more to the fore. To a woman, however, she will present above all the aspect of the terrible mother' (Hurwitz 2008: 31).

In *Daughters of Darkness*, Bathory shows both of these faces, which appear at different times during the developing plot, regardless of the gender of the person she is faced with. This sits in line with her bisexual and androgynous nature. Initially, in her plan to get to Valerie, she presents her sexual side to Stefan, in order to break down his defences. Once he is weak, she is able to strike. It is then that Bathory sets her sights on his attractive young wife — although Valerie puts up a lot of resistance to Bathory's sexually aggressive side.

Kümel employing the seductive vampire model — the divine whore aspect of Lilith — isn't unusual at all in this respect. Furthermore, if we take into account the fact that the director was intentionally making an erotic film, it becomes unavoidable. But, as with most things concerning the film, the approach used isn't typical, given that Bathory sends her agent, Ilona, to do her dirty work when it comes to actual sex, and seduction for the countess, more often than not, takes place — at least on the screen — on a more intellectual metaphysical level, thus avoiding the usual cliches of erotic cinema of the period as far as Bathory's character is concerned.

It is the other aspect of Lilith, the terrible mother, that lends *Daughters of Darkness* its edge over other films of its type. While Lilith can be seen as an ancient archetype of the vampire — and indeed the femme fatale, which will be discussed later in this chapter — this other side is far more horrific. It is said that Lilith would steal babies in order to suck the marrow from their bones, and according to Hurwitz, charms would be worn by pregnant mothers to ward off her evil presence (much like the vampire and traditional crucifix; although it must be noted that *Daughters of Darkness* offers up no such solution for defeating Bathory). This position goes against the grain of everything we are made to believe about femininity; women should be maternal and nurturing, not destructive takers of life.

In *Daughters of Darkness*, Bathory's other 'face' is that of the devouring mother, making her very much an incarnation of Lilith's duality. In several scenes Bathory displays a nurturing persona when she is playing out this aspect; the maternal face is a facade though, under which the potential for great evil lurks. It's a trick, and a very nasty one at that. For example, she comforts Ilona early on in the film, and the girl is presented lying in her master's lap, as the countess gently caresses her much like a child would lay with its mother. When Ilona is murdered by Stefan, Bathory snaps into the position of control, and both Stefan and Valerie become children in the situation; lost, in need of guidance and comfort from the dominating mother figure. It's almost like a mother who is helping her children cover up and fix a bad deed because she knows, deep down, they didn't mean it. Again, it's a sham, because her motivations are entirely selfish in nature.

Bathory dictates how to remove the body, clean up, and how to dispose of it, all while drawing Valerie into her care, as a comforter, posing as a safe parental figure. It's another form of seduction, just less obvious than one which uses sexuality. Part of the reason this works is Delphine Seyrig's age, and the fact that the actress decided to play the part 'all smiles'. Under this guise she takes on an outwardly maternal persona at key points in the developing plot. In adopting Valerie, much like an orphaned child (this is also helped by the fact that any sexual connotations are kept lurking in the subtext, simply suggested), especially after Stefan is killed, Bathory becomes her mother. But she is the devouring mother, who literally consumes her child from the inside out, simultaneously giving birth to herself again, using Valerie's body as a vessel. The film ends on an ambiguous note, leaving viewers to wonder how many other times she might have regenerated like this.

Monstrous or devouring mothers are not remarkable when it comes to horror. In fact, later on in the seventies they would become even more prominent in the genre, through films like David Cronenberg's *The Brood* (1979), and Brian De Palma's *Carrie* (1976). But they are unusual in the vampire genre, which tends to focus much more on sex. In fact, the sexual aspect of Lilith is almost par for the course in any vampire film where the creature is female. Many of these films rest on the heady combination of sex and death to sell; bringing motherhood into the equation risks killing the buzz. It's a difficult line to tread, but Kümel manages it with the aid of Seyrig's wonderfully nuanced performance.

When it comes to those films concerning Bathory specifically, the only title that comes close to possessing both aspects of Lilith is *Countess Dracula*. But in that particular film the countess is neither motherly or nurturing; she is fully monstrous, and has her own daughter kidnapped. Yes, Countess 'Dracula' may have consumed her daughter in a metaphorical sense, in that she steals her daughter's identity to carry out her wicked plan, but the plot leaves it there. In *Daughters of Darkness* Kümel pushes much further, ensuring Bathory eventually eats her young in order to survive. In no other vampire film made during this period, or indeed before it, do we see the terrible mother aspect of Lilith appear like it does in *Daughters of Darkness*. There are very few films, apart from perhaps *The Hunger* (1983) and 2010's *We Are the Night*, that have dared to delve into the territory since. Even those films do not touch on the devouring aspect of the terrible mother, instead using maternal behaviour as a mentoring function, and as a means of manipulating younger women who have, or are about to be, turned into vampires themselves.

HEAVENLY CREATURES: CARMILLA AND THE ROMANTIC VAMPIRE

Given the fact that Carmilla has overtaken Countess Bathory when it comes to cinematic female vampires, it comes as a slightly ironic twist that Le Fanu's forerunning text may have been influenced partly by the countess's story; or at least this could be the case, according to Matthew Gibson in his 2007 article 'Jane Cranstoun, Countess Purgstall: A possible inspiration for Le Fanu's *Carmilla*'. Gibson proposes one of the author's sources for ideas could have been William Sabine Baring-Gould's *The Book of Were-wolves* (1863), stating:

> This work drew attention to Wagener's earlier researches into Erzsebet Bathory, the Hungarian Countess who killed her female servants in order to rejuvenate herself with their blood, but who, in Wagener's account, clearly drew pleasure from inflicting sadistic sexual humiliation on her victims, 'especially if they were of her own sex'. The newly current story of Countess Bathory therefore helps to explain why Le Fanu's vampire is a lesbian as well as a Hungarian Countess. (Gibson, 2007)

Carmilla in itself drew from numerous sources, and there has been much speculation as to what these are. One point where scholars do agree is Le Fanu is likely to have taken from Coleridge's unfinished poem, Christabel, which Gibson (2007) describes as 'the first ever lesbian succubae poem in the English language', in the aforementioned essay.

Coleridge's poem 'Christabel' was written between 1797-1800, but was never finished. A proposed further three parts failed to surface, leaving the story incomplete. The prose that does exist takes the form of a complex winding narrative, in which the titular character Christabel encounters an escaped kidnap victim — or at least this is what she is led to believe — a young girl, named Geraldine, whom the former invites into her family home to take refuge. The poem comes loaded with notes of lesbianism — although not explicit — which is a key feature in Le Fanu's *Carmilla*. It is also suggested that Geraldine is a sinister figure, which is noted in the line that describes the girl undressing, before she lies down with Christabel: 'Behold! her bosom and half her side… A sight to dream of, not to tell!' This particular line has been interpreted as meaning Geraldine bears a horrible kind of mark or disfiguration, the nature of which is never explained but could signify she is an agent of evil. Overall, the passages in which Geraldine enters Christabel's bedroom have an unsettling atmosphere with the indication something terrible is about to happen. As the story develops, the girl is welcomed into the family home and Christabel's father develops something of an infatuation with the newcomer.

In addition to the lesbian flavour, there are other parallels to be found between Christabel and Carmilla. For instance, the idea something evil is hidden the guise of a young girl, who is able to inveigle herself into the safe haven of a family unit and then exploit the situation. Similarly, there is the line of obsession, or infatuation, which surfaces in both texts, suggesting the vampire, or succubus in the case of Christabel, has the power to manipulate the emotions of her victims.

Carmilla tells its story mainly from the position of the young female protagonist Laura who, just like Christabel, takes pity on another girl who she believes is in trouble. This girl, who becomes a cuckoo in the nest, Carmilla Karnstein, is introduced when she is involved in an accident with her carriage outside Laura's home. Laura convinces her father to allow Carmilla to stay with them to recover, while the Karnstein mother (who is also travelling in the carriage) has to rush off on business. However, the girls' closeness becomes unhealthy and obsessive, and Laura starts to develop an illness, weakening over time, while she is tormented by dreams that an animal is trying to attack her in her sleep.

Just as Coleridge informed Le Fanu, you can then see a definite progression of some of the themes found in both pieces of work in Kümel's film. Most notably these revolve around the idea of an outsider penetrating the family unit. In the case of Valerie and Stefan, Bathory essentially becomes the third wheel in their fresh marriage, and while it is important to highlight the idea of a vampire coming between a newly wed couple is likely to be derived from Stoker's novel, the reason Valerie is able to succumb to the Countess — despite resistance — follows more in line with Le Fanu.

In *Carmilla*, Laura is vulnerable because she is lonely. Her mother has died and she has no female company. She lives on an isolated estate with her father, who is loving but cannot fulfil her need for female companionship. Laura is desperate for a friend. This explains why she falls so easily into the predatory Karnstein's arms. Valerie in *Daughters of Darkness* shares a similar isolated existence to Laura. Although she has Stefan, as the plot progresses he becomes increasingly emotionally distant. Valerie has nobody else to turn to, even when he starts beating her, until Bathory makes it clear, through insistence and aggressively pursuing the girl, that she is there for her. One gets the idea, from quite early on, that it's only a matter of time until Valerie's resolve will crumble, and that resistance is futile.

Through subtext we are also fed the idea that Valerie is desperate for an extended family. She speaks little of her own background, only to indicate she considers herself a lower class to Stefan, with his supposed aristocratic heritage. She sees meeting Stefan's mother as a matter of urgency, and it is her insistence that he makes this happen as soon as possible that appears to drive the initial wedge between them. It is odd that a woman on her honeymoon is so keen to break up the intimacy she has with her husband at the quiet seaside resort, in order to pursue her place in his family home. Stefan's resistance only seems to cause resentment for Valerie. This implies, while never overstated, that Valerie could be searching for a mother figure, because she doesn't have one of her own. Acceptance into the family is a key concern for her, far more, in fact, than consummating her marriage.

Once again, we are brought round to the idea of motherhood. In *Carmilla*, Laura is also looking for a mother figure, and Le Fanu's interloper plays that part, just as much as she does the lover, in order to take maximum advantage of her victim. Likewise, in *Daughters of Darkness*, Bathory also fulfills this role, and just as Carmilla, she uses it to consume her prey, adapting a suitable face, lover or mother, to fit whatever Valerie might need at any given moment. And it is the combination of lesbian sexuality and maternal coercion, which bonds *Daughters of Darkness* and *Carmilla* on a subtextual level.

FLOWERS OF EVIL: DECADENT VAMPIRES AND THE FIN DE SIECLE

Moving beyond Gothic, Kümel's film displays a direct allegiance to the genre's darker, more heavily sexualised stepchild, French symbolism, through its decadent, yet cynical, celebration of sex and death, when twinned with aspects of lesbianism and transgression. In 1857 Charles Baudelaire's *Les Fleur du Mal* (*Flowers of Evil*) a collection of 101 poems — which had originally been titled 'The Lesbians' in its draft form — not only provoked an obscenity trial when it was originally published, resulting in three of his poems being banned, but it was a book which went on to both highlight and define the cultural malaise inherent in the era known as the fin de siècle (a time period which spanned the latter years of the nineteenth century).

The fin de siècle was much more than a collection of years. Ledger and Luckhurst define the period as of one of turmoil and great change, where the traditional and modern clashed in opposition, calling it 'a time fraught with anxiety and with an exhilarating sense of possibility' (Ledger & Lockhurst, XIII). Victorian tight-laced morality was challenged by the developing transgressive cultural movement — art, writing and music — that sought to rip open the metaphorical corset of traditional values, spilling open the contents to reveal and revel in the darker side humanity: illicit sex, drugs, immorality and decadence. Europe was in the midst of a spiritual crisis, after Christian values were eroded by scientific advances made during the Enlightenment. As a result, those who could afford it turned to libertine pursuits and occult ritual as a way of relieving the existential boredom they felt — otherwise known as ennui — in order to make sense of a world which was rapidly changing around them. Many artists of the period embraced a sense of nihilism, cynicism and pessimism, as much as they did freedom and modernity.

Baudelaire's text marks a turning point in this cultural revolution. In describing the aftermath of the writer's trial, Jonathan Culler proposes, 'More shocking, though, to nineteenth-century readers than scenes of love between women [three poems in *Fleur du Mal* concerned lesbianism; two of which were prosecuted], which had occurred in both pornographic "serious" literature, was the linking of sex with sadism and death in The Flowers of Evil' (Culler, 1993: xviii).

Although this combination of sex and death was also an aspect found in Gothic, especially the texts of Stoker and Le Fanu (*Dracula* and *Carmilla*), Baudelaire's work was far cruder and more explicit, as demonstrated in the poem 'A Carcass' where lovers discuss a corpse they encounter, and the prose is heavily sexualised:' Her legs were spread like a lecherous whore/Sweating out poisonous fumes/Who opened in slick invitational style/Her stinking and festering womb.'

Moving beyond the shock value of Baudelaire's prose – and the book was truly shocking for its time – there is much more to be found lurking beneath the surface than just corpses with spread legs. *Les Fleur du Mal*, and many of the books which followed it, also redefined female sexuality in a literary sense. The pages of Baudelaire and his peers warned that women were no longer submissive to men, they were now dangerous, world-weary, powerful creatures, in charge of their own sexual urges, and totally enlightened when it came to knowing how to use sex as a tool for manipulation. As Cullers explains, remarking on the change in content of the book, from the original lesbian exclusive concept:'In shifting from "The Lesbians" to *Les Fleur du Mal*, Baudelaire moved from a classical setting to a modern one, and, in essence, replaced lesbians with prostitutes as his representative female figures — figures, who, like lesbians, do not find satisfaction in relationships with men. What persists through these changes is the lack of symmetrical sexual relations between men and women' (Culler, 1993: xvii).

Lack of symmetry when it comes to sex and gender is one of the key aspects of *Daughters of Darkness* which makes it distinctively different from many of its peers — placing it in a very exclusive camp of female vampire films, amongst the likes of Franco's *Vampyros Lesbos*, and Stephanie Rothman's *The Velvet Vampire* — which belong firmly in the tradition of decadent writing, maybe more so than they do in Gothic.

For example, Jules Barbey d'Aurevilly's *Les Diaboliques* — d'Aurevilly was a staunch defender of Baudelaire — presented another collection of stories which revolved around the notion of sexually powerful women, who dominated and tormented their emasculated and weak male counterparts. The main theme of the book is denoted in the iconic line, 'The Devil teaches women what they are – or they would teach it to the Devil if he did not know'. Likewise, Joris-Karl Huysmans' heady exploration of satanism in nineteenth century Paris, *Là-bas* (1891) uses an unscrupulous sexually-motivated female character, Madame Chantelouve, to lure the central protagonist down into depraved depths of the Parisian underworld, where he is stripped of his moral compass by manipulation and seduction at the hands of a cold, calculating woman.

It's interesting that adaptations of decadent writings such as these remain largely absent from mainstream genre film. Yet, their spirit is evident in features like *Daughters of Darkness*, making the film all the more special for its rare allegiance to a long-forgotten genre of literature, at least as far as cinema is concerned. One exception to this rule is the work of writer Jean Lorrain, whose short story 'A Glass of Blood' became the basis of Jean Rollin's 1979 film *Fascination*.

Lorrain presented some novel takes on vampirism throughout his work, moving the concept beyond Gothic formula and into a more overtly sexual and decadent French symbolist framework. For example, in 'The Egregore' — one of the short stories in his collection *Sensations et Souvenirs* (1895, published in English as *Nightmares of an Ether Drinker*), from which Rollin also took 'A Glass of Blood' — the vampire is linked strictly to same-sex relations:

> The Egregore... attaches itself only to its own sex, entirely in contract to the ghoul, incubus or vampire. Their malevolent work is self-explanatory; it is with their kisses, with the accursed fire of their knowing caresses that they melt the flesh and the heath of the living like wax... It is the unfeeling and deleterious influence of a creature of darkness, of a dead man or a dead woman that instals itself beside you in the guise of a living one, insinuating itself into your life, your habits and your admirations, meddling with your heart and taking odious root there, while its damnable mouth breathes fatal passion into you. (Lorrain, 2016: 11)

This idea of 'insertion' into one's life seems particularly relevant to *Daughters of Darkness*, when you take into account this is exactly the way in which Bathory is able to infiltrate, and then later claim, Valerie, by inserting herself, quite literally, into her victim's unraveling marriage. It is with 'kisses' and 'knowing caresses' that Bathory is able to ensnare Valerie. Seduction is carried out as a long game, where every moment of entrapment and cruelty is savoured, as Bathory takes 'odious root' by Valerie's side in order to inflict her 'fatal passion' on the girl.

In Lorrain's 'Funeral Oration', from the same collection, the narrator tells of his friend's descent into depravity, and untimely death, when he takes up with a female ether addict who slowly drives the man insane. This story becomes pertinent in relation to the model of the femme fatale, which will shortly be discussed in this chapter.

Meanwhile, 'A Glass of Blood' links blood drinking with lesbianism, the main focus being a young woman who is treated for a blood disease, most likely anemia, who is given a treatment which involves drinking ox blood to restore her health and vitality. The stepmother waits for the girl to return from one such session, but the text describes this period as one longing for a lover, rather than anything concerned with maternal affection. Furthermore, the idea of blood on lips which are then kissed is used as an erotic device. In essence the story transgresses sexual and familial codes of normality, while mixing the themes of sex and death. Here again we see the appearance of a mother/lover as seen in both *Carmilla* and Kümel's film, although Lorrain is more explicit than Le Fanu or Kümel dare to be in this regard, drawing a concrete line to incest through legal family ties.

In *Fascination*, director Jean Rollin expands on the central theme of drinking animal blood found in 'A Glass of Blood' to present a cult of female cannibals, who may or may not be supernatural vampires. The film has much in common with *Daughters of Darkness* when you consider the power and class dynamics involved in the basis of Rollin's cult. These are rich society women, who kill strictly for fun. Women who are able to use the guise of femininity to lure, and then feast, on men of a lower social class; men they view as nothing more than fodder in their murderous games. Rollin's female cult are Sadeian libertines, just like Countess Bathory in *Daughters of Darkness*, for whom nothing, not even love, will get in the way of drinking blood and taking life. Love and sexual obsession, in both films, leads to ultimate destruction of an object of desire. Themes of companionship, possession, and warped love, which often appear in other vampire films of this type, are replaced with the idea of consumption and total annihilation. This message is made even more transgressive by the fact that the aggressors in both films are females, who are neither excused or punished for their crimes.

Femme Fatales and Blue Angels: Countess Bathory and Marlene Dietrich

Moving back to Lorrain's 'Funeral Oration' — a lament for a man driven into drug abuse and death by his sickly obsession for a depraved woman — or even the devil women of d'Aurevilly, and Huysmans' nefarious Madame Chantelouve, what we see emerge from decadent writing is the model for what we now know in cinematic terms as the femme fatale. Early incarnations of this character type were dubbed 'vamps' in silent era cinema, perhaps not surprisingly, given their vampiric qualities: the ability to strip a man of his life, sometimes in a real sense leading to death; sometimes by destroying his work or family, through systematic manipulation via sexual coercion. In this framework, male logic and morality are no match for primal desire, and men, at least under these circumstances, become the weaker sex. It's the ultimate castration nightmare where men are crushed and emasculated by sexually powerful women.

While there are similarities to be found between the two, the vamp or femme fatale is distinctly different from the Gothic or mythical vampire, and therefore can be seen as a progression of the Gothic character which removes supernatural aspects, to instead present a harder, more driven and selfish model fit for morality fables set in the modern world. For this reason it is perhaps understandable that while femme fatales do appear in horror film, their occurrence is more likely to be linked to thriller or drama genres such as the film noir.

Daughters of Darkness does something special in this regard. The film manages to simultaneously present a mythical vampire — through the supernatural angle — and a femme fatale, in a classical cinematic sense, which is achieved through Kümel's intentional link to cinema's golden age, by modelling Bathory on icon Marlene Dietrich, and Ilona on one of the definitive cinematic vamps, the original lost girl Louise Brooks.

As discussed in Chapter One, Kümel's decision to base his vampires on golden age Hollywood icons was initially based on economy. With a period film proving cost prohibitive the director had no choice other than to set *Daughters of Darkness* in modern times. His innovative work around, using the style of cinematic icons, was more than a happy accident though. Kümel could have picked any actress from the 20s or 30s, but the fact it was Louise Brooks and Marlene Dietrich carries with it a very specific subtextual element, which in turn lends greater depth to the characters, and, in the case of Bathory, provides a further link to a decadent tradition.

Actress Delphine Seyrig studied one of Dietrich's iconic roles before acting in Kumel's film, Josef von Sternberg's *Shanghai Express* (1932). In the film, Dietrich, described as a 'coaster', plays a prostitute who travels up and down the Orient, funding a lavish lifestyle through a series of affairs with wealthy men, whom she drives mad, and ruins in the process. The character, Shanghai Lily, after a failed love affair, has become cynical and hard (although as the narrative develops so does her softer side). It is the world weary attitude, summed up in such dialogue as 'it took more than one man to change my name to Shanghai Lily', that most reflects in the character played by Seyrig. Bathory, just like Lily, is a nomad, constantly on the move. Moving from place to place she seemingly latches on to victims and drains them dry. With Bathory this occurs in a literal sense; for Shanghai Lily it's more in a financial and emotional sense. At one point, Lily and her companion (played by Anna May Wong) are described as 'having no souls' by a doctor who is aboard the train they are travelling on, thus delivering a direct link to vampire tradition — vampires are also thought to be lacking in this department. The doctor explains the women are, 'riding this train in search of victims'. As he explains, 'That Shanghai Lily, for the last fortnight I've been treating a man who's out of his mind after spending every penny on her'. Slightly later, when quizzed on her respectability, Lily replies, 'Don't you find respectable people terribly dull?' Seyrig appears to have taken inspiration from this as she delivers Bathory's line, 'Nothing in life is ever serious'. The words might be completely different, but they exhibit the exact same ballsy, decadent spirit.

On a stylistic level *Daughters of Darkness* pays further homage to *Shanghai Express*. Seyrig studied Dietrich's overstated dramatic gestures (a commonplace way of acting for stars who had previously appeared in silent film) and mimicked some of this for the role she played for Kümel. For instance, the way in which Bathory arrives at the hotel is a direct reference to von Sternberg's film. Bathory's face is lit in Rembrandt lighting, obscured under a veil, when she first makes an appearance from her car, as *Daughters of Darkness* cinematographer Eduard van der Enden replicates the visual feel of *Shanghai Express*. Seyrig then makes a determined stride to the hotel lobby, modelling her walk on Dietrich's.

Likewise, some of Seyrig's costumes would not have looked out of place on Dietrich — lavish sequinned gowns, huge feather boas while the French actress' hairstyle comes very close to Dietrich's in *Shanghai Express*. In similar fashion, for Ilona, actress Andrea Rau styled her hair on Louise Brooks' famous 'It Girl' bob. Brooks, who made a name in silent era cinema, had her biggest success away from Hollywood when she starred in two films by Austrian director G. W. Pabst: *Pandora's Box* (1929) and *Diary of a Lost Girl* (1929). However, like Seyrig's incarnation of a vampiric Dietrich, the association between character and star moves beyond a simple visual statement. In the two aforementioned films, and especially *Diary of a Lost Girl*, Brooks, while demonstrating she is capable of abandoning moral values in order to survive, as central protagonist Thymian, is very much a product of her environment, and someone who is chewed up by a series of unfortunate events in her life. Ilona is from the same stock. She is able to use sex, when needed, but also, is largely victimised by the stronger, more callous and manipulative Countess Bathory.

In this way the vampires in *Daughters of Darkness* move beyond simple stylisation into the realm of pure cinema. The associated visual aesthetic involved in constructing Bathory and Ilona deliberately uses fashion and gesture as a pure cinematic language, thus instilling a series of specific contextual meanings, which indicate the inner nature of the characters, without having to resort to explanation through dialogue.

Epilogue

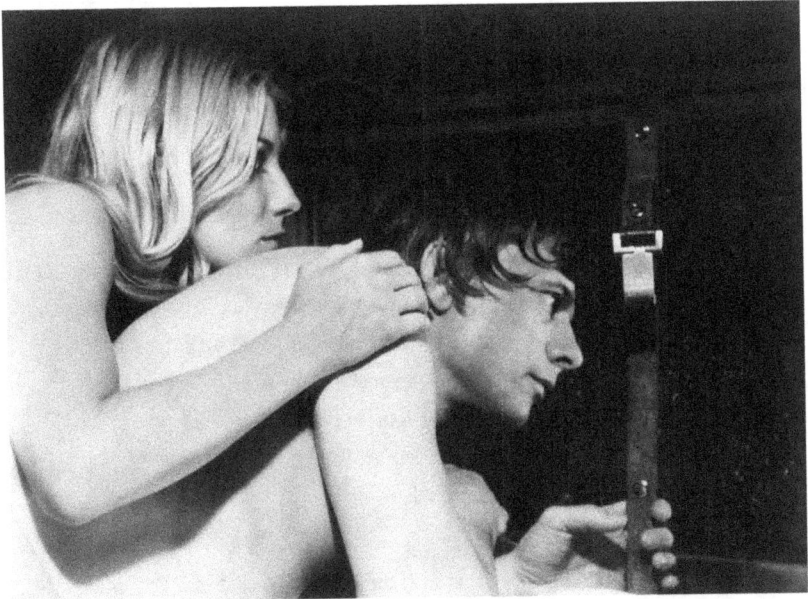

By the seventies the landscape of vampire film was changing radically. *Daughters of Darkness* fits neatly into this shift. In 1975 Stephen King would publish *Salem's Lot*, a contemporary American Gothic novel which he described as 'Peyton Place meets vampires' (King, 2005: 4). King wanted to remove what he felt were Stoker's 'optimistic' elements from the Dracula myth, and bring the story to a modern setting, to instead reflect the cynical atmosphere of his own time. The author, who started the novel in 1972, just a year after *Daughters of Darkness* was released, explains, 'mine was a world that had begun to choke on its own effluent, that had hooked itself through the bag on diminishing energy resources, and had to deal not only with nuclear weapons but nuclear proliferation' (ibid.). In King's novel, the vampire becomes the destructive antihero, and it could be argued that this followed a trend partially set by Kümel's film.

This sense of pessimism and cynicism runs rife throughout seventies vampire film. Even Hammer horror got in on the act with *The Satanic Rites of Dracula* (1973), bringing the vampire into a contemporary setting and making him an overlord of capitalism. Other films, such as *Hanno Cambiato Faccia* or *Thirst*, discussed in Chapter Three, employed a similar metaphor. In addition, many critics have argued Cronenberg's ultra-modern take on vampirism, *Rabid* (1975), used the figure as a reference to venereal disease. George A. Romero's *Martin* (1977) delved into the notion of masculinity and sexuality in a rapidly changing cultural climate, from the point of view of a socially isolated, and possibility psychotic, young man.

Daughters of Darkness has an allegiance to many of these films in the way in which it channels the cultural climate of the period and gives vampirism a modern slant. As shown in this book, the film's heritage angle directly links to a trend evident in some of the other genre cinema of the period, especially that which critiqued capitalist and class-driven facets of society. However, as much as *Daughters of Darkness* shares a kinship to films like *Thirst*, and is also influenced by the cultural malaise of the decade, it is also unique in its status as a progenitor of what Camille Paglia termed 'psychological high Gothic', which, according to Paglia at least, can be defined as 'A classy genre of vampire film' (1990: 268).

Although Paglia rejects Tony Scott's *The Hunger* on the basis that its central vampire is too animalistic, the film does have its place in the story of *Daughters of Darkness'* legacy. Catherine Deneuve's sophisticated cultured queen vampire Miriam (Deneuve, like Seyrig, is an actress also heavily associated with French arthouse cinema) shares many of the same traits that Countess Bathory displays: a love for the finer things in life, proclivity for female companionship, a manipulative personality compelled to force others into becoming her companion to fulfil her need to be adored, despite the fact it will cause suffering to those who are chosen. Similarly, Miriam is shown to groom her disciples, as does Bathory, and uses the same mother/lover means of exploitation to get what she wants.

In the decades that followed, while it was not a huge trend, more psychological high Gothic began to appear on the scene. In recent years intellectual, or so called 'elavated' vampire films such as *Kiss of the Damned* (2012) and *Only Lovers Left Alive* (2013) appear to draw from the spirit of Kümel's original feature, while 2008's *We Are the Night* combines the energy of millennium action/horror cross-over films like *Blade* (1998), with a framework concerning classy lesbian vampires. That particular film focuses on a tough, streetwise young woman forced to use crime as a means to survive, who is then groomed by a trio of vampire women wholly decadent in their behaviour and lifestyle. Once again we see the emergence of an older matriarchal vampire figure who is glamorous, intelligent, calculating and cruel, in line with the tradition started in a large part by Kümel.

When reflecting on the legacy of his film, and its position in the arthouse bracket, Kümel finds the acclaim of *Daughters of Darkness* somewhat ironic:

> It was not an arthouse film, it played on 42nd Street at that time in New York. And you know what 42nd Street was in the seventies, it was one of the worst parts of New York. It's not like it is nowadays. And it played in erotic cinemas and people took it at face value. Nowadays, well there were people who considered it already at that time, I remember I was shooting *Malpertius*, and the great actress who was in *Malpertuis* said, 'Ohh, it's marvellous, the film, the colours!'. When it was shown at the MOMA [Museum of Modern Art] in New York, later, they were raving about it. But it was far from being an artistic movie. It made millions in France, played everywhere, in seventy countries, which for a Belgian movie is unheard of. It is was done without one cent of official money.

It seems Kümel has not has his last word on Countess Bathory yet, and intends to add another piece to the legacy himself by producing another film, although he is quick to add it is 'not a sequel, but a revamp'. All he will say on this matter at the time of writing this book is,

> It will be Bathory of course, another actress, and it will have the same set of characters more or less, but completely changed, but it has the same kind of inspiration. It will be filmed on a ferry going from Belgium to Britain and then the main part will take place in Bradford, in Yorkshire. The only tip of the veil I can lift for you is that in Bradford is the Midlands Hotel, and in the Midlands Hotel the great British actor Henry Irving in 1905 died. And the manager of Henry Irving was none other than Bram Stoker, the writer of *Dracula*, who was also a theatre manager. In the confusion of the death Bram Stoker abandoned his luggage at the hotel. I was invited to go to Media Museum of Bradford, which no longer exists, and I saw that luggage and I thought ahh, that is perhaps the trigger for a new movie... voila!

DEVIL'S ADVOCATES

References

Carter, Angela (1978) The Sadeian Woman and the Ideology of Pornography. New York: Pantheon Books.

Cherry, Brigid (2014) 'Vampire Aesthetics and Gothic Beauty'. In Brode, Douglas & Deyneka, Lena (eds) (2014) *Dracula's Daughters: The Female Vampire on Film*. Maryland: The Scarecrow Press.

Craft, Kimberly (2009) *Infamous Lady: The True Story of Countess Erzsebet Bathory*. South Carolina: Createspace.

Culler, Jonathan (1993) Introduction, notes on the text, selected bibliography published in Baudelaire, Charles (2008) *The Flowers of Evil*. Oxford: Oxford University Press.

Forshaw, Barry (2013) *British Gothic Cinema*. London: Palgrave Macmillan.

Frayling, Christopher (1992) *Vampyres: Lord Byron to Count Dracula*. London: Faber & Faber.

Gibson, William (2007) 'Jane Cranstoun, Countess Purgstall: A Possible Inspiration for Le Fanu's "Carmilla"'. *Le Fanu Studies 2*. At http://www.lefanustudies.com/cranstoun.html (Accessed 31 May 2017).

Harris, Jason Marc (2008) *Folklore and the Fantastic in Nineteenth-Century British Fiction*. Abingdon: Routledge.

Hurwitz, Siegmund (2008) *Lilith: The First Eve: Historical and Psychological Aspects of the Dark Feminine*. Einsiedein, Switzerland: Damion Verlag.

Keesey, Pam (1997) *Vamps: An Illustrated History of the Femme Fatale*. Minneapolis: Cleis Press.

Kümel, Harry and Gregory, David (2016) Audio Commentary, *Daughters of Darkness*. Blue Underground.

Lee, Christopher (1977) *Tall, Dark and Gruesome*. London: Granada Publishing Limited.

Lorrain, Jean (2016) *Nightmares of an Ether Drinker*. Sacramento, CA: Snuggly Books.

Mathijis, Ernest (ed.) (2004) *Cinema of the Low Countries (24 Frames)*. London: Wallflower Press.

Noakes, Lucy (2006) *Women and the British Army: War and the Gentle Sex*. Abingdon: Routledge.

Paglia, Camille (1990) *Sexual Personae*. New Haven, Connecticut|: Yale University Press.

Perrault, Charles (2012) *Two Tales by Charles Perrault: 'Puss in Boots' and 'Bluebeard'*. A.J Cornell Publications (Kindle edition).

Thorne, Tony (2012) *Countess Dracula: The Life and Times of Elisabeth Bathory*. London: Bloomsbury Paperbacks.

Todorov, Tzvetan (2018) *The Fantastic: A Structural Approach to a Literary Genre*. New York: Cornell University Press.

Towlson, Jon (2016) *The Turn to Gruesomeness in American Horror Film 1931-1936*. Jefferson, North Carolina: McFarland & Company.

Williams, Tony (1981) 'Feminism, Fantasy and Violence: An Interview with Stephanie Rothman', *Journal of Popular Film and Television* 9, no 2. Summer 1981: 84-90.

Zimmerman, Bonnie (1981) 'Daughters of Darkness: Lesbian Vampires', *Jump Cut: A Review of Contemporary Media*, no 24-25, March 1981, pp 23-24.

Zimmerman, Bonnie (2015) 'Daughters of Darkness: The Lesbian Vampire on Film. In, Grant, Barry Keith (2015) *The Dread of Difference: Gender and the Horror Film*. Austin, Texas: University of Texas Press.

www.ingramcontent.com/pod-product-compliance
Lightning Source LLC
Chambersburg PA
CBHW071414300426
44114CB00016B/2301